FASHION CHINA

FASHION
CHINA

GEMMA A. WILLIAMS

286 illustrations, 253 in color

Thames & Hudson

p. 2 Dress, Chictopia, SS14.
p. 7 Xander Zhou, SS11.
pp. 14–15 Chris By Christopher Bu, 'Double' collection, SS14.

First published in 2015 in paperback in the United States of America by
Thames & Hudson Inc., 500 Fifth Avenue, New York, New York 10110

thamesandhudsonusa.com

Library of Congress Catalog Card Number 2014944632

ISBN 978-0-500-29164-1

Printed and bound in China by Shanghai Offset Printing Products Ltd.

CONTENTS

FOREWORD

Hung Huang

HUNG HUANG IS A TV HOST, WRITER AND INFLUENTIAL MEDIA FIGURE. AS THE PUBLISHER OF GROUND-BREAKING FASHION MAGAZINE *iLOOK* AND REGULAR WRITER FOR *WOMEN'S WEAR DAILY* SHE HAS BEEN PERFECTLY PLACED TO WITNESS THE TRANSFORMATION IN CHINESE FASHION. HER BEIJING STORE, BRAND NEW CHINA, HAS ACTIVELY SOUGHT TO PROMOTE THE WORK OF HOMEGROWN DESIGNERS.

Working at the leading edge of the publishing industry since the 1990s, I have witnessed first-hand the sheer determination and flair of the key players who are transforming fashion in China. Transitioning from a closed climate with little choice or individualism, the field of fashion in China today has now opened up as a ground for experimentation and possibility. It is so exciting to see talented and aspiring designers increasingly feel the confidence to launch themselves on the fashion circuit, as more and more Chinese brands and labels are established.

With my own publication, *iLook*, I was perfectly placed to provide a platform for the emerging designers who were breaking new ground with innovative models of production and design, and to disseminate these across the Mainland. By opening a retail store, Brand New China, in 2010 I could provide a physical space in which to sell and promote these enterprising young designers, allowing them a space to develop. I am proud to say that my team and I saw very early on the potential of Chinese fashion, for a Chinese market.

I must say that Gemma Williams should be credited for great foresight in creating this anthology of Chinese designers. It is true that the general market in China still prefers international brands, but thanks to people like Gemma and a handful of expatriates, young Chinese are beginning to recognize their own brands and learning how to express themselves through local fashion.

Showcasing some of the best fashion brands and upcoming designers operating today, this book will act as a bridge to introduce these brands to a worldwide audience. Compared with when I started out in fashion, the industry in China is now thriving and it will only be strengthened by this publication. It is a truly dynamic time for Chinese fashion and a most relevant time to capture the thoughts and accounts of the people who make up the design industry at this very moment. It is also timely to recognize those Chinese designers working internationally, who are studying and interning abroad and choosing to start brands outside of China. *Fashion China* provides an insight into a fast-paced, energetic and still largely latent market to which all fashion fans can look with expectation.

INTRODUCTION

China is a country like no other. Its sheer scale, diversity and complexity elude simple description and analysis. Similarly, its contemporary fashion landscape is diverse and diffuse so that few people outside China are aware of the dynamic developments taking place within its burgeoning fashion industry. Even inside China many are unaware of the new designers working hard to establish the reputation of their 'Designed in China' labels.

This book introduces the very best and most exciting Chinese designers working today. Some are based in China's fashion capitals of Shanghai and Beijing, while others operate from more remote locations within China's borders. Still others have chosen to set up their labels abroad, often after training overseas. From ready-to-wear to couture, womenswear to menswear, and from well-established commercial enterprises to newcomers more interested in aesthetic experimentation than mass appeal, the labels that appear in this book all have one thing in common: they are transforming the reputation of Chinese fashion, at home and abroad.

The current dynamism of China's fashion industry is all the more fascinating given the country's complex history and complicated relationship with art and design. For over 5,000 years, China has been a civilization renowned for its highly skilled craftsmen and artisanal traditions producing luxurious decorative arts and textiles. Its transition to a Communist state, however, meant many areas of both practical and cultural output became regulated. The focus became function rather than form, on the object rather than the individual who designed or produced it. As a result, a domestic fashion industry did not come into being until the late 1980s, following economic reforms and the opening up of Mainland China to international trade.

The subsequent and exceptionally fast-paced social and economic changes recast China as a global superpower. The corresponding development of a fashion infrastructure was swift and unprecedented – however, not necessarily design-led. China became known as the workshop of the world, and over time the label 'Made in China' became synonymous with low-quality, mass-produced items.

In stark contrast, today, a wave of driven and enterprising designers is pushing forward the still nascent scene. Young, talented and ambitious, they have founded labels that seek to redefine the traditional connotations of what it means to be 'Made in China'.

Previous page: Masha Ma, AW12.
This page: Chictopia, 'Circus Concept' collection, SS12.

It is credit to a growing number of Chinese consumers that these labels are flourishing. With ever-increasing spending power, Chinese shoppers are beginning to look beyond international fashion houses and luxury brands to embrace homegrown talent. Stores stocking only Chinese labels have sprung up to fill – and increase – demand. Boutiques such as Brand New China and Dong Liang in particular have been pivotal in supporting independent designers. Their efforts to introduce and promote Chinese fashions as an alternative to established European brands have had an enormous impact on what products are now available to the Chinese consumer. In their wake have followed established multi-brand retailers such as Galeries Lafayette and Lane Crawford, which are now stocking and promoting Chinese brands alongside their international ranges. Wealthy patrons are also beginning to realize the potency of fashion to promote and revive the best of Chinese culture. The Chinese appreciation for their heritage and art is now being channelled into purchases and commissions of locally designed and made textiles and fashion.

China's contemporary fashion landscape orbits around its two fashion epicentres, Beijing and Shanghai, each with its own clustered fashion scene and biannual fashion week. Other less likely and more isolated cities are also slowly becoming hotbeds of creativity, for example Xiamen and Guangzhou in the southeast. In a development that is creating greater synergy between China and the wider world, some designers are choosing to base their operations abroad, often after completing degrees at design colleges worldwide. Increasing international study is felt to not only complement the more technical emphasis of China-based training, but also to enable students to address their Chinese heritage and identity in a global context.

The influence of tastemakers and well-known personalities has taken on a new importance in promoting indigenous fashion; their choices can result in the overnight success of local brands. The creation of a fashion press over the last few decades has also been instrumental in constructing a space for fashion within the Chinese psyche. Local companies such as Modern Media and publications like *Harper's Bazaar* China and *Vogue* China have introduced an engaged and interested audience to fashion history in the West, while also showcasing homegrown designers alongside global brands. Chinese fashion now competes with the best on the red carpet, in magazine editorials, films and at international fashion weeks.

Due to the timely development of the industry, brands can take full advantage of the range of purchasing platforms now available in order to reach the lucrative domestic market and beyond, to international customers. The relative youth of many Chinese designers also makes them more keyed into the opportunities afforded by e-commerce and social media. The work of Chinese designers is now being shown on the runways of the big four fashion weeks in New York, London, Milan and Paris. The truly global strategies that have resulted would have been impossible just a few years ago.

Advances in Chinese manufacturing standards have meant that the materials and fabrics available to designers producing within China are better than ever before. More and more textile manufacturers are catering to this specialized demand, working with brands to trial and create bespoke fabrics. But there is still room for improvement. For the Chinese fashion industry to build on its current momentum, manufacturers need to commit to helping local designers pioneer new and innovative materials. They too can only benefit from establishing the infrastructure needed for the fashion industry's continued growth.

In curating the selection of designers featured in this book I was helped in no small way by a panel of industry experts, each at the forefront of his or her respective field (see page 12). Their unique insight into the swiftly evolving Chinese fashion industry and collective experience in its various arenas has been invaluable.

The designers and brands featured in this book form a snapshot of the fashion industry in China as it stands today in all its varied forms. Together they reveal an ambition and determination that will undeniably ensure the continuing development of a strong and vibrant national industry that will drive fashion trends in China and in the West. For the first time, China is now firmly on the international fashion radar and its designers' emphasis on quality, innovation, tradition, concept and craftsmanship looks set to guarantee its very bright future.

CHEN MAN

KARCHUN LEUNG

As a representative of modern Chinese visual artists and photographers, Chen Man has built her own visual language. Her solo exhibitions have been held in France, the US, the UK, Japan and Hong Kong, and she has also participated in significant art fairs. The V&A Museum in London, MoCA Shanghai and Today Art Museum in Beijing have collected her work. Chen Man is pioneering a revolution in contemporary fashion and art photography.

Karchun Leung is a Hong Kong-born fashion journalist currently living in Shanghai. He began his career in newspapers and has also worked as a visual merchandiser for ITHK, giving him valuable retail experience. After working for *City Magazine* Hong Kong, he moved to Shanghai to become the Deputy Chief Editor for *Modern Weekly*. He is now the Chief Editor of *Numéro China*.

THE PANEL

THE AUTHOR HAS CURATED THE SELECTION OF DESIGNERS INCLUDED IN THIS BOOK IN COLLABORATION WITH THESE FOUR INDUSTRY EXPERTS, EACH WORKING AT THE FOREFRONT OF THEIR FIELD. BETWEEN THEM THEY REPRESENT IMAGE-MAKING, EDITING, STYLING AND MODELLING, AND THEY HAVE BROUGHT AN UNPARALLELED LEVEL OF EXPERTISE TO THIS COLLECTION.

LUCIA LIU

LIU WEN

Born in 1983, fashion stylist Lucia Liu lives and works in Beijing and London. She founded her own styling studio in 2010 and was appointed Style Director of *Harper's Bazaar* China in 2011. Her quality work and creative thinking have contributed a significant change to the magazine. Lucia has also become one of the most sought-after and trusted stylists among celebrities and brands.

Discovered in 2005, model Liu Wen has made waves throughout the fashion industry, collaborating with renowned photographers and brands. She was the first Asian spokeswoman for a global cosmetics company (Estée Lauder), the first Chinese model to walk for Victoria's Secret, and is noted by American *Vogue* as having 'the biggest social-media audience of any model'. In 2012, *The New York Times* named her 'China's first bona fide supermodel'.

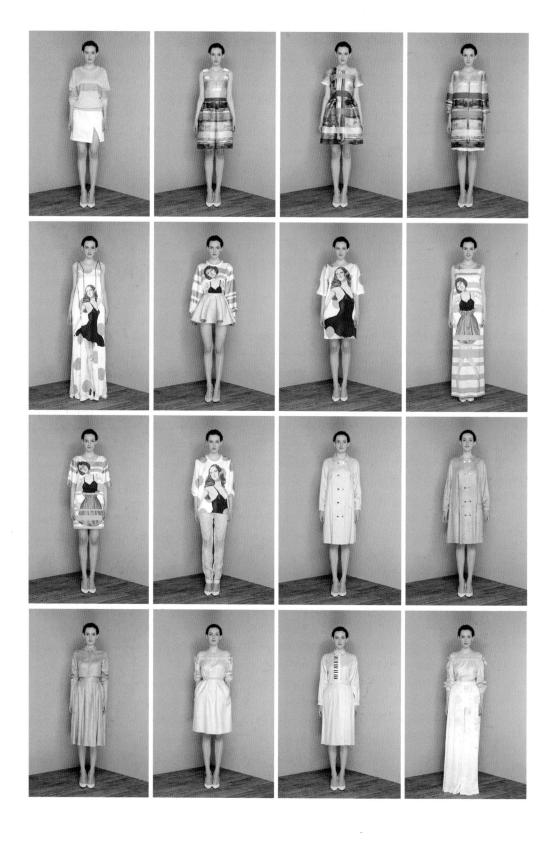

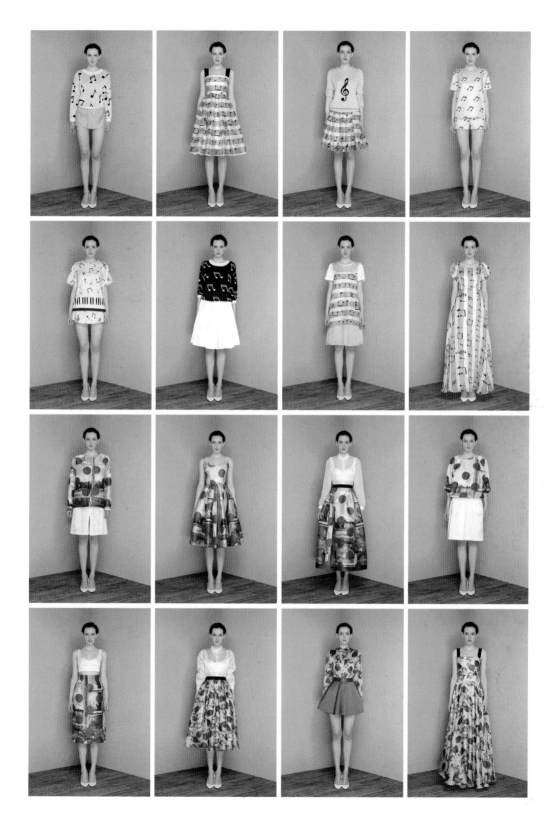

BABYGHOST

SINCE ITS INCEPTION IN 2010, BABYGHOST HAS BEEN THE GO-TO BRAND FOR MANY OF CHINA'S MOST KNOWLEDGEABLE TRENDSETTERS. BASED IN DOWNTOWN MANHATTAN, DESIGNERS JOSH HUPPER AND QIAORAN HUANG ARE AT THE HELM OF THIS TRULY MODERN BRAND. WITH THEIR FASHION-FORWARD IMAGERY, ACCESSIBLE PRICING AND ABOVE ALL DESIRABLE CLOTHING, THEY ARE MAKING THEIR NAME KNOWN ON BOTH SIDES OF THE GLOBE.

The name of your label is an unusual construction, a combination of differing ideas. Is this also applicable to your design concept? We knew from the beginning that we wanted to invent a word rather than use anything eponymous. Actually, our name came quite naturally. There is a lot of contrast between our backgrounds and we felt 'Babyghost' was the perfect expression of that. We were fortunate to both work as assistants under the same designer prior to starting our label, which gave us a year of learning how the other person approached and solved design problems. It's safe to say that the only real difference between us now is the perspective that our gender lends to our process. Other than that we pretty much think as one.

As a duo, how do you divide up the design process and resolve differences? Intuitive exploration! We follow our feelings and are constantly exchanging design roles. At times one of us feels like sketching or draping, and at others maybe we both just want to spend the afternoon at the cinema. Which is perhaps the soul of any organic design relationship. We usually resolve our (design) differences by a fight to the death! In all seriousness, anyone who claims that conflict is not part of their process is selling the process short. Conflict is what creates everything around us. Sometimes we do argue, and the result is always the same: what is right eventually rises to the top, and being true to our intuition is something that we both agree is paramount in our choosing which of us is *right*.

How does being based in New York influence your label and what are the advantages of the city? New York City gives anyone a lot of perspective. We love it for the clash of race, culture, lifestyle and energy. However, we actually travel for most of the year and with each city we visit we find something new to fall in love with. In this day and age we all have the sensation of living everywhere. The Internet really changed the whole game and now it's not so much about what city your studio is in as much as it is about where you find your inspiration.

What do you think of street-style and casualwear in China? *Qiaoran*: When we talk about street-style we think of it more in terms of which social network we're using at the moment. We see all these amazing looks that people take on the street and then post online. Especially for the younger generation in China, the Internet is really changing the way they approach their day-to-day style on the street. *Josh*: LOVE IT. Talk about fresh eyes! China is both ready to make a statement, and unconditionally in love with their past. It's damn exciting to take in and process when we are travelling and working in China. Something like watching the evolution of a peacock in fast-forward!

Your label is fashion conscious and design led but well priced. Who is your ideal client? Our ideal client is the type of girl who wants to feel a solid emotional connection to the clothing that she chooses. Who enjoys sharing an affinity with the work that we do, and can see that we are making an effort to speak directly to her when we are designing. In the beginning we wanted to create a collection that had the same accessibility as the music we buy on iTunes. We wanted to

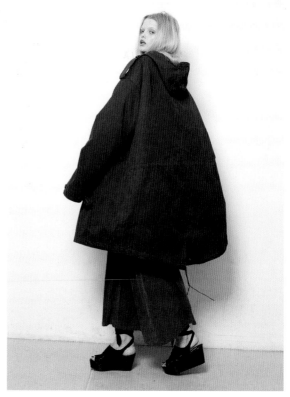

reach the largest audience that we could and intentionally tried to keep our pricing at a level that would be easy for most people to buy into. When we design we think a lot about our friends and fans. We like combining their different tastes and predilections with a sort of fictional girl that we create each season.

You have received considerable press support and have some notable Chinese patrons from the modelling industry in particular. How important is it to have brand ambassadors who you feel are a good fit for the label? It's always important to share a lot of common ground with the people who help represent your brand. Just like our name, the following that we have also came pretty naturally. We rarely have to ask our friends to wear Babyghost for a photo. If someone requests a garment we give it to them with love and they are often photographed. We believe that combining a passion for what you do with pure intention has great power in this world.

Where do you think the brand currently sits within the fashion industry and how do you hope to develop as designers? Well, we're probably sitting at a table by ourselves at the moment! As for our development as designers, it's really been the most fascinating four years of our lives. As our business grows so does technology and with it access for our fans to all our innermost thoughts and inspiration. Our social network really pushes us with every collection to step up our game and is in many ways providing an entirely new process for designing clothing. For instance, whereas five or six years ago there were mood boards, now there is Instagram and WeChat on our smartphones. Through these applications we feel an almost instant connection to what the people who purchase our clothing want.

Page 16: SS01.
This page: Looks from AW12.
Opposite: SS13.

'Our social network is in many ways
providing an entirely new process for
designing clothing'

BAN XIAOXUE

THIS TALENTED DESIGNER MAY OPERATE OUT OF THE INDUSTRIAL POWERHOUSE OF GUANGZHOU BUT HIS UNIQUE, CONCEPTUAL DESIGNS ARE ENTIRELY INSPIRED BY NATURE. AN EMPHASIS ON MATERIALS, TEXTURE AND STRUCTURE RESULTS IN PARED-DOWN, STRIKING SILHOUETTES. FOUNDED IN 2012, HIS LABEL WENT ON TO WIN THE PRESTIGIOUS INTERNATIONAL WOOLMARK PRIZE FOR CHINA THAT SAME YEAR.

Did you always plan to become a designer? In my university years I majored in Fashion Design. However, I seldom make plans for my future; instead, I'm accustomed to expecting the unexpected. All I can do is concentrate on what I'm doing at the moment, and attentively do my best.

Your mother worked as a seamstress. Did this influence your career path? My mother worked as a seamstress when I was very young, but that had no real impact on my profession. I did indulge in drawing at that time, and I began to draw some figures with costumes when mom took me to the tailor shop. She taught me to be simple and honest, so I have been accustomed to faithful design and expression without excessive and deliberate modification, trying to be as pure and natural as possible. This was the greatest influence of my mother on me.

How did you develop as a designer during your five years at pre-eminent Chinese brand Exception de Mixmind? During my five years at Exception I matured from design assistant to chief designer, and from designing single pieces with unconstrained and vigorous style to mastering the year-round design planning of the brand. With an attitude of diligence and the readiness to take on responsibility, I rapidly developed in a short period.

What made you decide to start your own label? It was actually purely accidental that I created my own brand, as the result of the requirements of the finals of the International Woolmark Prize. I created my personal brand Ban Xiaoxue upon getting through the regional championships within China. This has enabled me to embark on a much purer road of design.

What is your philosophical approach to design? I follow nature. All living things have their particular colour, texture and structure, and what I do is just make records. My inspiration changes with fluctuations in nature. The best design must be the one that moves the designer first, and only then is shared with others. Materials are one of the most important parts of my design, the most powerful language in design, and also the first step in design. I take my inspiration from nature.

Why is wool such an important material for you? To me, wool is like an old friend, we have known each other for a long time. It's exquisite and delicate, soft and comfortable, with great richness of quality. Wool also has many functional properties such as high breathability, good insulation and excellent elasticity. The importance of wool in my works lies mostly in its versatility, which has allowed me unlimited use of my imagination. The interactions of wool with other materials have rendered me innumerable possibilities: cosy or sleek, thick or lithe, delicate or unruly, flamboyant or plain.

What innovative techniques and treatments do you employ with wool? We place importance on developing new techniques that demonstrate originality and a sense of memory and occasion. With wool, we start by designing the single yarn in wool weaving, then we change the degree of twist, thickness and evenness, before finally redesigning the weaving organization to create changes in the texture of the wool.

You were the China winner of the International Woolmark Prize. How did this help your brand and what mentoring did you receive? Thanks to the Woolmark Prize, Ban Xiaoxue has managed to genuinely enter the international stage and share our understanding of beauty. The support and recognition has enabled us to have the confidence to firmly continue our path.

Nature is a strong influence on your work. How important is your environment when you are designing? I lived in the country surrounded by rivers and mountains, so I gained a sense of intimacy towards nature, which can be seen in the garments I design. My collections are marked with purity. Beautiful things grow in nature, rather than being created by humans. We can only discover the beautiful things, not create them.

How do you feel about this new movement in Chinese design? For me, this is a natural phenomenon, and there is no need to deliberately think about 'fitting in'. As we were born into and grow up in this era, we naturally belong to it.

What would you see as the benefits for a label currently operating in China? It's a great time for brands in China at the moment, in terms of market tolerance and customer acceptance. Under these circumstances, brands will gradually mature and form their own unique orientation and features. From the perspective of the overall international atmosphere, more and more attention has been given to Chinese labels, rendering greater confidence and impetus to Chinese designers.

What motivates you? There are two things that motivate me. One is to follow my dream and the other is to overcome the challenges set by myself and by reality. I believe that people cannot live without a dream, big or small. With a dream, you have the power to push on and deal with every difficulty. Yet challenging yourself is also key to achieving any dream. Only by stretching yourself to the extreme will you overcome your own limitations and the dilemmas that real life brings you.

Opposite: 'Spontaneous' collection, 2014.
This page, overleaf and page 23: 'Growth'
collection, 2013.

'There is an old Chinese
saying that one's handwriting
reveals his personality, and
so it is with clothes, too'

<u>This page:</u> 'With Belief, Hope and Love' collection, 2014.

BOUNDLESS

ZHANG DA, THE DESIGNER BEHIND THE LABEL BOUNDLESS, RUNS HIS ATELIER FROM SHANGHAI. HIS CONCEPTUAL APPROACH TO CULTURE AND THE APPLICATION OF DESIGN MARK HIM OUT AS ONE OF CHINA'S MOST RESPECTED FASHION DESIGNERS. HIS GOAL WITH EACH DESIGN IS TO BREAK NEW GROUND AND BRING ENJOYMENT TO THE WEARER. THROUGH THIS LABEL HE AIMS TO SHOW WHAT HAPPENS WHEN FUN IS INJECTED INTO DESIGN.

What impact do you think international education and new technologies are having on the new wave of Chinese designers? An international education gives students access to better training on basic techniques. It is very beneficial to gain a better understanding of the European and American fashion industries, cultures and working habits, and mastering another language. For Chinese designers, the greatest benefit of new technologies is the change in retail channels, namely e-commerce, which enables independent designers to start their business and realize their design and commercial goals at a relatively low cost. This has triggered significant changes in China.

You have spoken about the two phases to your work, the combination of the conceptual with the practical application of design. Can you tell us more about your specific approach to design? There are in fact three working methods in my design: 1) Abstracting the rules and common grounds from the materials that I'm interested in, and then applying those rules to my own designs and further developing them. 2) Collecting interesting objects from everyday life and different cultures, studying their craftwork and functional designs, and rearranging the culture and messages in them to obtain new visual and cultural meanings. 3) Setting a goal, which is far-fetched or seems unachievable. Then, through design and craftwork, I find a way to realize that goal.

Are enough designers approaching fashion from an intellectual viewpoint? It is not enough to design only from the intellectual perspective, because besides the intellectual part, the emotional part of fashion design and pure visual enjoyment are also important. The person in the dress should obtain satisfaction from every aspect.

Do you see your design process as an ongoing continuation of fashion history or something new that pushes practical and theoretical boundaries? A part of my design method is a continuation of history, because it is very hard to create a brand-new method of design, or make an outfit that has never appeared before. However, I hope through my design work, a new aesthetic and method can be derived from the extant system, and this is one of my goals.

Your work has been exhibited internationally. Do you ever design with the museum in mind? When I design a dress I only consider the situation when it is worn by a person, rather than exhibited in a museum.

Since you have been working in the industry how have you seen the fashion media in China develop? China's history of fashion communication goes back less than thirty years. During that time, fashion media has been developing rapidly in paper, online and mobile media. However, the depth, reliability and diversity of fashion communication are disappointing. Flamboyancy, superficiality, and the singleness of values and aesthetics are abundant in China's fashion media.

What are your future plans for Boundless? I hope I can avoid the fast-working pace of the fashion industry, but can also survive and create interesting products.

'For me, fashion is a means for self-expression to convey my cognition of the world'

Opposite left: Detail, padded coat, AW14.
Opposite right and below: Backstage, AW14.

Above: Dress, SS05.

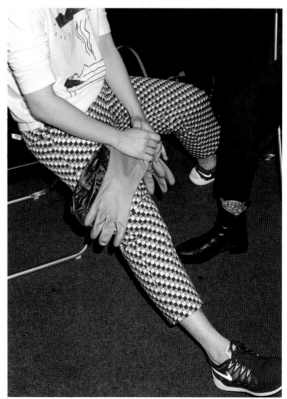

This page: Catwalk, AW14.
Opposite: Padded coat, AW13.

CHICTOPIA

AT THE AGE OF JUST TWENTY-FOUR, BEIJING NATIVE CHRISTINE LAU STARTED WHAT IS FAST BECOMING ONE OF CHINA'S MOST POPULAR BRANDS, CHICTOPIA. HER COMBINATION OF FLATTERING CUTS, QUIRKY AND STRIKING PRINTS, DIGITAL EMBROIDERIES AND VIBRANT COLOUR PALETTE HAS ENSURED MAXIMUM ATTENTION FROM THE WATCHING FASHION INDUSTRY. THE BRAND HAS ALREADY BEEN PICKED UP BY HIGH-PROFILE STOCKISTS AS WELL AS INTERNATIONAL ONLINE PLATFORMS.

Where does the name Chictopia come from? Chictopia comes from the words 'Chic' and 'utopia'. It represents dreams and idealism of fashion.

When did you decide to start a fashion label? I decided to start a fashion label in the final year of my BA course in textile design at Central Saint Martins in London.

There is a constant stream of exciting brands emerging from Beijing. How important is this city as a base? I think Beijing is now the best city to start a new brand in China. First of all, there is an arty atmosphere and it is the cultural centre of China. Secondly, Beijing is the centre of the fashion and media industries. Thirdly, it is a big market and consumers are eager for new things. Plus, Beijing is my home and I feel more comfortable working here.

How difficult was it to set up your brand? It was extremely difficult to set up my brand because back when I started five years ago there were no fashion buyers in China. No shops would carry indie designers' products. My only option was to open my own shop. Production was another problem because, due to the small quantities of my products being produced, few factories would take on the work.

What did you gain from studying abroad? This was the most important decision for my design career. The atmosphere of Central Saint Martins was very inspiring and I met many interesting and creative people from all over the world. The tutors were also good at inspiring me.

Your prints and cuts often play with humour. Are Chinese people open to humour in fashion and who is your ideal client? Yes, they are very open to humour in fashion. My ideal client is a girl who is self-confident and playful.

Which Chinese designers or eras in Chinese design inspire you? I am particularly inspired by a number of designers who started their brands in the 1990s. I think they were the first generation of Chinese indie designers, and some of their labels have gone on to become highly commercial brands.

Your brand has been picked up by many high-profile retailers including international online stockists. Why do you think your design is making such an impact? I think because my unique style is highly memorable. I also believe that my products achieve a good balance between design concept and commercial needs.

What is your design and manufacture process? There are fifteen people in my team working on design and manufacture. We usually look for materials first, then we start to design our own fabrics and do samples, which may include different techniques such as dying, printing, jacquard, knitting and laser cutting. At the same time, we will work on shapes by pattern making and draping on mannequins.

Where would you like to see your brand in five years? I would like to become a mature local brand and have some global exposure.

Previous page: Picasso dress, SS14.
This page and opposite: Looks from SS14.

This page: Christine Lau.
Opposite: Bai Baihe wearing Chictopia, SS13.

CHRISTOPHER BU

AS A GRADUATE OF THE BEIJING FILM ACADEMY IT IS PERHAPS NOT SURPRISING THAT CHRISTOPHER BU'S COUTURE GOWNS NOW GRACE THE RED CARPET TO GREAT ACCLAIM. HIS COLLABORATIONS WITH ICONIC ACTRESS FAN BINGBING IN PARTICULAR HAVE MADE A NOTABLE IMPACT FOR THEIR USE OF TRADITIONAL CHINESE SYMBOLISM. NOW WITH A RETAIL SPACE NESTLED AWAY IN A TRADITIONAL *HUTONG*, HIS READY-TO-WEAR LINE, CHRIS BY CHRISTOPHER BU, OFFERS A MORE CONTEMPORARY SENSIBILITY AT A FRACTION OF THE PRICE.

Not many stylists make the crossover into design. What inspired your own transition and why do you think it has been so successful? I love fashion and design with all my heart and I dedicate most of my time to it; the passion really keeps me going forward. I don't think I have really achieved success yet as I'm just at the start of a long journey, but I have been blessed to have so much help and love, which means a lot to me.

How has your training impacted how you approach or think about design? I have a habit of picturing my designs in certain scenes in my mind because of what I studied. I think it's a lot of fun for me to do this during the process, just like I'm telling a story.

Fan Bingbing has worn two of your creations to Cannes. How important was this platform for show-casing Chinese design and what exactly was your desired message? It was such an honour for me that she chose to wear my designs on this hugely significant platform. I'm a big fan of ancient Chinese history and culture, which carries very different messages from its Western counterpart. I would also like to show the world, especially the young people out there, real Chinese craftsmanship since it's somehow getting harder for people to see this through the process of globalization.

How does your creative collaboration with Fan work? She has always been a big risk-taker, and we have been working together for many years, and sharing similar thoughts in terms of styling and fashion. We are both huge fans of ancient Chinese

costumes. When we are not working we just sit down and talk about what I want to do, and she gives me her opinions. If she ever took a role in a film set in ancient China, she would turn to me for suggestions about the costumes.

In contrast to couture the focus in your diffusion line, Chris by Christopher Bu, is on wearability, with a very playful approach to print. How and why did you identify these as your key signatures? I love to dress young girls who are happy and want to have a little bit of fun in life, and I hope the girls who wear my designs can be easily identified in the crowd. That's part of the reason that I chose playful prints in most of my designs for the diffusion line. I think I will stick to that in my future designs.

Going forward, do you ever plan to incorporate your interest in history and heritage into your diffusion line as you do in your couture? I definitely want to show-case Chinese culture and heritage in my future designs, finding a way of balancing ancient aesthetics and modern silhouette.

High-quality fabrics are integral to your brand. Where do you source them? From the very beginning, I have been lucky to work with friends with similar interests to be able to develop my own fabrics and maintain the uniqueness of my garments. The majority of Chinese textile manufacturers ask for big orders, which I cannot satisfy.

Do you work with a print designer to develop your prints? Yes, I have a group of friends who help me realize the

prints that are in my mind. We work together really closely, I tell or show them what my inspirations are and what I want, and they develop the prints according to that. It's always a long process since it needs repeated communications and modifications.

How do you interpret your aesthetic in terms of other Chinese brands currently operating? For my design, I put a lot of emphasis on wearability and personality by giving a little bit of a twist to the classic looks through the combination of playful prints.

How important is it to you to be stocked in multi-brand stores such as Brand New China? The multi-brand boutiques such as Brand New China have their own very loyal customers, which new designers like myself really need. They offer platforms where new designers are presented and new labels are promoted. We have been working with many boutiques in China.

Why did you choose London as inspiration for your SS13 launch collection? London is a magical place for me. I fell in love with it right away when I went there for three days' work. But I decided I wanted to stay longer, so after finishing my work I cancelled my original return tickets. I ended up spending nearly a month in London, where the avant-garde blends into the ancient. I went shopping, sightseeing, flipping through weekend markets. I love the stories the city tells.

This page and overleaf: 'From London With Love' collection. SS14.
Opposite: Suit inspired by plant specimen. AW14.

'I put a lot of emphasis on
wearability and personality'

COMME MOI

LV YAN HAS BEEN A WELL-KNOWN FACE IN CHINA SINCE LAUNCHING HER MODELLING CAREER IN THE 1990S. SHE HAS NOW TURNED HER TALENTS TO DESIGN AND RECENTLY LAUNCHED HER OWN SHANGHAI-BASED LABEL, COMME MOI, SPECIALIZING IN AFFORDABLE LUXURY. HAVING LIVED IN PARIS FOR MANY YEARS, SHE TAKES FRENCH INFLUENCES AND TRANSLATES THESE INTO CLEAN LINES AND CRISP TAILORING.

Do you have any formal design training and what is your personal design philosophy? I don't have any formal design training. It would certainly be a plus if I had and I'm naturally working very hard now to learn as much as possible to 'fill the gaps' and to acquire the necessary skills. Yet, I'm lucky to work with an amazing team from whom I'm learning a lot. Comme Moi design is the result of teamwork and I'm simply the creative director of the company. I don't have a design philosophy at this early stage of my career as a designer. I just try to select beautiful fabrics and to produce well-shaped clothes that make women feel beautiful and confident in their daily lives.

What made you decide to start Comme Moi? I'm very intuitive and emotional: I decided to start Comme Moi because I'm genuinely passionate about fashion and design. I'm also a people-person and I know a great deal of talented, creative and visionary people in the industry in China, Paris and New York. I think I wanted to stay close to and work with this network of friends and potential partners with whom I had such a great time over the past years. I was probably also looking for new challenges and ways to express myself further.

You have been working in the fashion industry for many years. What major changes you have experienced over the years? I believe that one of the most striking changes that I have experienced over the past few years is the democratization of fashion. Luxury and high-end design is no longer treated as 'sacred' and nowadays everyone can be fashionable. You don't have to spend a fortune now to buy great clothes or accessories. Fashion is now less elitist, which is probably a good thing. In China, more specifically, I notice lately that women have learnt to sharpen their taste, to form their own aesthetic and to define their own style.

As the brand evolves what would you like it to become known for? I would like the brand Comme Moi to be known for what I'm trying to offer: 'affordable luxury' for young, sophisticated women! I would like people to say: 'this brand is cool, sexy, easy-going yet always chic'.

Given your previous work as a model, do you pay particular attention to the body and its relationship to the garment? This is exactly where I see the connection and the logical path between my experience as a model and my new endeavour as a designer! I believe it is extremely important when designing to visualize how the garment will react to movements and motions. I insist every day on making sure that our designs work with the lifestyle of a modern urban woman.

What typifies Chinese design for you? I'm not sure that there is a common ground between all Chinese designers apart from the ethnicity and some cultural heritage that goes with it. I used to believe that Chinese designers had a strong focus on ornaments and an excessive desire to demonstrate their tailoring skills, resulting in complex pieces. Comfort or wearability didn't seem to be a priority. Now, though, I see designs that are far simpler, in clean shapes and subdued colours.

How well do you think the wider fashion industry supports emerging labels in China and could more

Opposite and page 47: Lv Yan wearing AW13.

be done locally to promote Chinese design? I actually believe that the 'wider fashion industry' is doing quite a good job supporting emerging labels in China. For instance, I learnt recently that some garment manufacturers are now considering developing local brands and are scouting for talented designers. I personally have met with local investors seeing great potential in Chinese new ready-to-wear labels. I also see more and more multi-brand stores opening and some specialize exclusively in new Chinese designers. I think the industry is eager to see the advent of strong Chinese brands.

What do you think is the importance of Chinese models on the runways? As everyone has noticed, there are more and more Chinese faces on the catwalks representing fashion brands worldwide. I guess it's the best way to appeal to the lucrative market of Chinese consumers, but I also think there are many Chinese girls chosen for their extreme professionalism. As Comme Moi is a Chinese brand I will certainly choose a majority of Chinese models for our shows.

Why are international perceptions of Chinese designers changing? When it comes to fashion or design, people still refer to Paris, Milan, New York and maybe a few other places as the key hubs. China is primarily seen just as a market, where brands want to be and to sell. However, great designers such as Alexander Wang and Philipp Lim are starting to change international perceptions. I also believe that people outside China know now that Chinese brands can produce high-quality designed products.

This page and overleaf left: Singer Li Yuchun wearing Comme Moi, SS14.

'In China I notice that women have now learnt to sharpen their taste, to form their own aesthetic and to define their own style'

<u>Above right:</u> Model Du Juan wearing Comme Moi, SS14.
<u>Opposite:</u> Lv Yan wearing Comme Moi, SS14.

DEEPMOSS

ONE OF CHINA'S MOST BEGUILING YOUNG DESIGNERS, CENTRAL SAINT MARTINS GRADUATE DIDO LIU PLACES THE SIMPLICITY OF HER CUT AT THE CORE OF HER AESTHETIC, AND TREATS CLOTHING AS A FORM OF SCULPTURE, TO BE VIEWED FROM MANY ANGLES. HER DEEPMOSS LABEL IS CONTROLLED AND ASSURED, AND HER WORK IS IMBUED WITH A DELIBERATION FAR BEYOND HER YEARS.

Where do you find your inspiration? My inspiration comes from the mundane and the everyday. It comes from any tiny experience that touches my heart.

What attracted you to Central Saint Martins as a design school? Before going to CSM I studied fashion design in Beijing for two years, where I honed my patterning and sewing skills. During that time I also met some graduates of CSM who encouraged me to study at what they considered to be the best fashion college in the world. I feel that CSM provided the opportunity for me to explore all kinds of designs: apart from clothes I designed headwear, bags and other products. As a student of Fashion Design with Marketing I also learnt about the importance of targeting consumers while designing.

How did you find your experience of studying in London and would you encourage other young designers to pursue this path? Yes, definitely. It teaches you to constantly rethink, to keep working hard and to be bold in your decisions.

What have you learnt since starting your label that is not taught in college or university? Everything! It's like being a soldier on a battlefield, where you have to learn to adapt to the situation around you, and you never know what you are going to be bombarded with next.

The theme of your brand is 'Youthful Old Soul'. Can you explain what you mean by this? 'Youthful Old Soul' was the theme from my first collection. I want to make clothes for young people but with a sophisticated and mature wisdom. I want this theme to also set the tone for the future development of Deepmoss.

What do you mean when you say you 'sculpt' your clothing? A garment must be viewed not just front and back. It is essential to examine every angle in order to design it.

With elongated proportions your silhouettes seem decidedly international. What is your distinctive approach to the body? I wanted to emphasize the soft and quiet side of my collection and I like to design with quite elongated proportions. I think that the body, especially those of women, should be soft, and that qualities of strength and power should be on the inside. All of this comes from my Chinese roots, which have a strong influence on my philosophy and aesthetics.

Your lookbooks conjure up a very self-contained world. Do you work with a stylist and how important is the look of the model in the representation of your brand? No, I am the stylist on my brand. I want to achieve poetry, romance, subtle detailing and to always be natural. The look must combine a contemporary feel with oriental aesthetics.

What are the main issues currently facing young designers in China? We have a huge domestic market but immature market systems, which limit the potential for young designers to reach Chinese consumers.

<u>Opposite and page 53:</u> AW13.
<u>This page:</u> Details, SS14.

This page and opposite: AW13.

'Inspiration comes from any
tiny experience that touches
my heart'

DIGEST DESIGN

IN THE FACE OF CHINA'S RAPID GROWTH, DIGEST DESIGN FOUNDER DOOLING JIANG IS DETERMINED TO STAND HER GROUND AND TAKE THINGS AT HER OWN PACE. SINCE 2008 THE BRAND HAS BEEN OPERATING FROM BEIJING, OFFERING CONCEPT-LED DESIGN, WHICH ADVOCATES THE IMPORTANCE OF CLOTHING IN EVERYDAY LIFE AND, PERHAPS MOST IMPORTANTLY, AS A MEANS TO ELEVATE THE SOUL.

Can you explain the concept behind Digest Design? I used the word 'digest' in our name because Chinese fashion is still in its infancy, so both designers and the consumers need to do some 'digesting'. This is a process for both the Chinese fashion industry as a whole and for me as an individual.

How has your background influenced your work? I am a very conventional Chinese person, probably as a result of my family tradition. My grandparents on both my father's and mother's side were in the army, and they lived through great upheaval and hardship in China. I was born in the 1980s and have grown up in the city. Though I am not as thrifty and industrious as rural kids, my grandparents' life experiences make me more willing to work humbly and to want to make a contribution to the world.

From where does your design aesthetic originate? My flat sense of design and organic aesthetic come from my love of nature and the aura of harmony. When I travel between the skyscrapers in the city I always lower my chin and look down, but when I go hiking in rural areas even the lowliest plant is able to attract my attention. Mother nature is my best teacher, and observing the trees and grasses in nature is my most effective form of practise.

What are the main differences between your ready-to-wear line and your artistic line? From the very first season I began to design my ready-to-wear collection and conceptual collections separately, because I don't believe that the expressions of conceptual designing and the essence of clothing can be achieved simultaneously. I don't want to consider clothing as a tool to convey concepts, and it's never easy to make a widely accepted dress with strong and recognizable style. Separating 'concepts' and 'clothing' enables me to express my views freely and also make wearable clothes.

Do you sketch or drape on the body? When I first set up my studio I maintained the habit of sketching to make the design in my mind clearer to my colleagues. However, after six collections I have largely replaced sketching with oral description. Only when I can't describe certain details clearly would I do some sketches as complement. Draping is currently the most important job for me. Draping on mannequins is the most direct way to feel the fabric and control the space between the body and cloth.

What does styling mean to you? When I design, I imagine the type of person who would wear these clothes. I do all of the styling of the lookbook myself at the time of shooting. It's not that styling is something that I care about particularly deeply, although I know it plays an important part in the fashion industry. Doing styling myself is more about having fun, rather than pleasing potential consumers.

What is your viewpoint on fashion curation? Although I don't create my conceptual collections for this purpose, I have been invited to show my work in many exhibitions, including one in Holland called 'The Future of Fashion is Now'. However, as a general principle, Digest Design doesn't want to be too involved in the critique of fashion or design; instead, we just

want to do our best as we take every step forward and express ourselves honestly.

Could you talk about materiality? Fabric plays an essential role in my design, and I think it's the same for every designer. Sometimes I deliberately choose to use lower-quality fabrics, as I prefer to challenge and explore the possibilities of common fabrics rather than top-quality Chinese silk or European cutting-edge fabrics. That said, there is one particular type of material that I do love to work with, even though it is expensive: the completely handmade traditional fabric. For example, in the summer of 2013 we used Xia clothes (a traditional Chinese handmade linen fabric) in our conceptual collection 'Crack'. My friends and customers will also recommend to me all kinds of materials, which are mostly from their hometowns.

Considering China's rapidly developing economy, what are your future plans for Digest Design? China's rapid development awes people. In a fast-growing industry such as this I choose to maintain my own standpoint, but this standpoint is not anti-industry or anti-fashion. For example, Digest does not create its products strictly according to the spring/summer or autumn/winter categories; instead, we create a winter/spring collection as this suits our own design pace. We also don't participate in independent show-rooms and fashion shows, not because we don't need them, but because I don't think Digest is mature enough to be exposed to such publicity.

What do you see as your biggest challenge? The biggest challenge is how to help people realize the importance of clothing in their everyday lives, and to discover that clothing is not just decoration, but, I believe, a means to becoming a better person. In traditional Chinese culture, clothing symbolizes people's life experience and the order of society. Clothing in China needs to regain this level of significance.

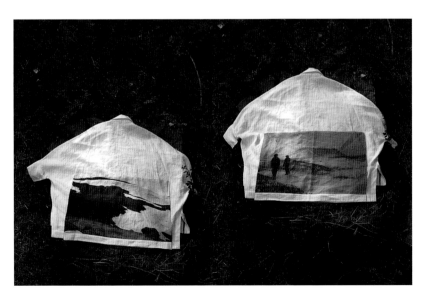

<u>Opposite, this page and overleaf:</u> Ready-to-
wear, 'Foundation' collection.

'To digest is one of our human
natures, while to design is a
product of modern society'

EVENING

FINDING INSPIRATION IN THE LITTLE THINGS IN LIFE, EVENING CREATOR YU WANNING HAS SHOWN HER COLLECTIONS IN BOTH BEIJING AND SHANGHAI, AND IN 2013 SHE WAS SHORTLISTED FOR THE ASIAN INTERNATIONAL WOOLMARK PRIZE. ORIGINALLY HAILING FROM THE NORTHEAST OF CHINA, SHE NOW CITES BEIJING AS THE CITY OF HER DESIGNS, AND HER ATELIER IS BASED IN THE CITY'S VIBRANT ART DISTRICT.

In the past you have made a point of incorporating leftover material into new designs. What is your definition of fashion? I use whatever materials meet the needs of my design, both natural and artificial materials. Fashion is about attitude; it is a clear and unique form of expression. I was born, raised and educated in China, and my designs are the result of this. They are my expression of the way I look at life.

You seem to experiment and develop with each collection. Do you see your design practice as an evolving process? I often refer to my design work as a complex sphere. Each collection is special in its own right, but together the collections create this multi-faceted sphere. I think that in the future my work will become bolder.

You trained at CAFA. How important was this choice of university and what are the main advantages of studying in China? CAFA is a very prestigious and highly regarded university in China. Many well-known artists have graduated from there. The first time I visited CAFA, while I was still in high school, I was captivated by it. CAFA's approach is a combination of a free and easy atmosphere with a rigorous professional approach, and this deeply affected me and has influenced my practices since.

Your atelier is based in 798, the art district of Beijing. How inspiring is this location and Beijing generally? While the 798 art district is in Beijing, it is also different from Beijing. Its physical landscape consists of a mix of old factories and contemporary sculpture. It fuses the old and the avant-garde and within it you can trace China's history while appreciating contemporary works. It has this kind of mixed temperament.

Do you think enough is being done to support young designers in China? Unfortunately, China's fashion industry provides very little support to young designers. Matters of production and processing can be very difficult, and the structure just isn't there to support newcomers. However, it is important to remember that we are still in the relatively early days of the industry in China and I believe this situation will get better in the future.

You play with prints quite a lot in your work. What do you think this injects into your designs? Printing is a way to design. I like the kind of abstract figurative expression that it allows. I think that the abstract form gives people more space and possibilities.

Can you tell me about your collection that included the ancient Chinese practice of Qigong? Wu Qin Xi is one of the oldest styles of the ancient health practice of Qigong, and is based on gracefully imitating the movements of animals. I wanted to use this as a design inspiration for a collection because I find the delicate relationship between humans and animals fascinating, and particularly sad when it breaks down.

What is your ultimate goal over the next five years? I want to continue to build on the existing work of Evening designs, and to continue to enrich the work we produce.

<u>This page, page 64 and opposite:</u> Catwalk looks from AW14.

<u>This page and opposite:</u> Backstage, AW14.

EXCEPTION DE MIXMIND

FOUNDED IN THE 1990S BY MAO JIHONG AND MA KE, EXCEPTION CAN BE CONSIDERED ONE OF CHINA'S FIRST ICONIC FASHION BRANDS. WHILE THEY ARE COMMITTED TO MAKING FASHION 'QUIETLY' AND DON'T ACTIVELY COURT PUBLICITY, THEIR WORK HAS NEVERTHELESS RECEIVED HIGH-PROFILE ENDORSEMENTS AND HAS A GROWING RETAIL PRESENCE IN MAINLAND CHINA. EXCEPTION PROMOTES AN EMOTIONAL AND CULTURAL CONNECTION TO CLOTHING, USING TRADITIONAL CRAFTS AND NATURAL MATERIALS TO ENRICH THE LIVES OF ITS WEARERS.

Mao Jihong, how would you describe the essence and identity of the brand? Exception captures the roots of culture in its designs. We allow our customers to find and express their Chinese cultural origins. We create clothing that is not dictated by fashion, trends or functionality, or any element of the external visual experience, but by inner feelings.

You were one of the first wave of students to study fashion design in China. Could you talk about this experience? When I enrolled at the Beijing Institute of Clothing as one of China's first generation of fashion designers, I had a dream: for everyone to be able to wear authentic Chinese brand clothing and use Chinese brand products, and to feel confident about our way of living.

Exception is based in Guangzhou. How important is this to the brand? Guangzhou has an open atmosphere, vibrant culture and government policies that are conducive to the birth and growth of enterprise. Guangzhou also has a relatively mature industrial structure. Exception was born here, and we want to absorb the city's cultural and artistic ideas, and incorporate them in our designs. However, we never limit ourselves to Guangzhou. We source materials from across China and globally: for example, Hangzhou silk and New Zealand superfine wool. We also know that reaching the consumer markets of Beijing and Shanghai is key to spreading our message.

When you started Exception in 1996, how different was the fashion landscape in China compared to now? When Exception was first established there was very little original design and creativity on the market, very few high-end brands, and Western aesthetic standards dominated. The birth of Exception reshaped contemporary Chinese women's fashion aesthetics and the way they dress themselves.

What inspires your design? As a student, I read fashion magazines and books nearly every day, and had my mind filled with colour and form, but I soon realized that those are just the surface of design. Real design comes from the heart, and I need to use words to enrich my mind. Music, books and even solitude and independent thinking are essential parts of the spiritual world that one needs to build in order to create a brand.

Could you talk about Exception's first fashion show? In 2004, Exception held our first public show, for the SS05 collection. The title was 'What We See Is What We Believe'. It was considered very avant-garde and rebellious at the time.

What role do traditional crafts and techniques play in your designs? Exception attaches great importance to the inheritance and development of traditional crafts, and we also believe that this makes us stand out from other brands. We have a technology department that specializes in hand-hook embroidery and knitting. We also have a research institution that works with Beijing Institute of Fashion Technology, specializing in the research and development of traditional costumes. We regularly employ techniques of Miao embroidery, so as to make traditional crafts a unique form of expression, which is very rare and valuable in the era of mass production.

This page: 15th anniversary catwalk show, 'A Love of Life' collection, SS11.

How is Exception using modern technologies to preserve and promote traditional techniques? We use a modern aesthetic consciousness to recreate traditional craft. Exception launched five laboratories in 2005, which are committed to researching cutting-edge technological developments in needle weaving, cashmere products, accessories, dyeing and finishing, and quality control.

You have said that you want to do fashion 'quietly'. What do you mean by this? This refers to a return to just-focusing on doing our own design. We don't consider more commercial issues, but do our work from the heart. As everyone knows, Exception does not do any advertising and rarely engages in any publicity work. We touch audience's hearts deeply through the product itself, the experience in the store and our special interaction.

You are currently planning to expand outside of China. Why is now the right time? Now is the best time for China's national self-confidence to establish itself and to show the world a new cultural identity. Exception is a representative Chinese clothing brand and the lifestyle and philosophy it advocates reflect the spirit of contemporary China. Exception will provide European and American customers with Chinese-style lifestyle products, while also promoting the Chinese way of life and way of seeing the world. This will be fresh and exciting to the international customer.

Opposite: 15th anniversary catwalk show. 'A Love of Life' collection. SS11.
This page and following page: First Beijing show. 'What We See Is What We Believe'. SS05.

'We create clothing that is
dictated by inner feelings'

<u>This page:</u> 'A Love of Life' collection. SS11.

FAKE NATOO

ZHANG NA IS THE DESIGNER WITH A CONSCIENCE BEHIND THE LABEL FAKE NATOO. A GRADUATE OF CHINA'S XI'AN ACADEMY OF FINE ARTS AND MOD'ART INTERNATIONAL IN PARIS, SHE HAS SETTLED IN SHANGHAI, WHERE SHE HAS BEEN RUNNING HER BRAND SINCE 2008. HAVING OVERCOME MANY OBSTACLES ALONG THE WAY, FAKE NATOO IS NOW EXPANDING ITS PROFILE ACROSS CHINA.

How important was your fashion design training at Xi'an Academy of Fine Arts in developing a design identity? I studied at Xi'an Academy of Fine Arts from the age of fifteen to twenty-two, and during that time I went through a serious and strict art training. On the other hand, this school time was romantic and full of freedom. That was an important period of my life, getting into literature, music and religion. But actually the traditional Chinese art education did limit my creative thinking to a certain degree. It was only after I studied in Europe and had worked for a few years that I started to question things. To this day I am still questioning.

Your garments feature a range of fabrics and materials including jacquards, natural fabrics and intricately dyed materials. How does your choice and combination of fabrication communicate your brand identity? Fabrication plays a crucial role in my design. Following my own personality, I tend to choose fabrics that naturally give me a warm and uplifting feeling. I want the wearer to feel cosy when they touch the fabric. I also love embroidery, print and recycled fabrics. For our AW14 collection, we used handmade yak-wool felt from a supplier based in a Tibetan area of Gansu province.

Who was your first stockist or early patron of the brand? How important was this support in helping you to forge ahead with your vision? In 2009, I did my first collection 'Shadow'. My first stockist was Seven Days, which was the only shop for Chinese independent designers at that time. That was an important step to begin, but soon they were caught in the economic crisis in 2009. I then decided to open a little 15 sq m shop with a friend on Changle Road, and while this later turned out to be a painful experience, it did mean that many people became aware of my label.

You collaborate with Tissu, an Italian fabric distributor, how does this process compare to sourcing Chinese fabrics? In fact, we do use a certain amount of Chinese fabrics, such as silk. But unfortunately a lot of Chinese suppliers cannot promise the same quality when it comes to production. There were two occasions in a row where I had to drive 400km in the middle of the night to deal with the factory, and still the result came out unsatisfying. On the other hand, with some high-standard Chinese suppliers the problem is that their minimum order is too much for an independent designer like me. I have worked with Tissu for many years and they understand me and always try to accommodate my needs in terms of making little alterations to their sample. The only concern would be time, it usually take two to three months to get the fabrics for production.

You are based in Shanghai but show your collections in Beijing. What are the differences between the two cities from a fashion perspective? Beijing is still the cultural centre of China, and that means more press exposure. Shanghai is more rational. The business environment is better. In the old days, a lot of big fashion showcases were in Beijing, but now most of them have moved to Shanghai.

Do you feel there are distinct and separate fashion scenes in these two cities or is there a form of mutual

support between the two? The two are very different, not only the physical city but also the people. China is very big, and the distance between Beijing and Shanghai is the equivalent of the distance between some European capital cities. I am from Beijing but I live in Shanghai and I think the two cities are complementary in terms of the fashion industry. They both have unique aspects, but have a mutual dependence when it comes to this industry.

Would you like to design for other brands? I love the German brand Bless very much. Their attitude towards life is very like mine. But for now I just want to focus on Fake Natoo. I really enjoy building up my own design language and exploring all possibilities.

Do you enjoy the challenge of running a label? I used to feel that I didn't want to run a business. I thought about finding a business partner, because it needs a completely different brain. But, after running the label for years, my thoughts changed. I realized that the creative and business roles are actually complementary. I started to understand people more and come to enjoy the process.

What are you currently working on outside Fake Natoo? I also have another label called Reclothing Bank. We make new designs from secondhand garments. Reclothing Bank is a separate project from Fake Natoo, but they both have the same value to me. I hope that they are the best gift I can give to this world.

Opposite: AW13.
This page and page 81: AW14.

'Fabrication plays a crucial role in my design'

FFIXXED

FIONA LAU AND KAIN PICKEN ARE THE DRIVING FORCES BEHIND THIS COLLABORATIVE ART PROJECT, WHICH STARTED LIFE AS A FUSION BETWEEN FASHION AND FINE ART. AS RECENT FINALISTS OF THE 2013 INTERNATIONAL WOOLMARK PRIZE SELECTED BY, AMONG OTHERS, TIM BLANKS AND FRANCA SOZZANI, THEY ARE COMMITTED TO CRAFTING A LIFESTYLE BASED ON A NEW UNDERSTANDING AND APPRECIATION OF DESIGN.

ffiXXed began as a project combining design and art and you took some years to experiment and develop your aesthetic. What influence has this process had on your approach to fashion and when did you feel ready to commit to fashion? ffiXXed has always been about exploring new ways to live and work together. We began ffiXXed as a way to produce a more cohesive framework through which to do this. Our approach has always been very open and fluid and this continues to influence the way we work with the label, both in terms of how we work together but also with regard to our approach to materials and how we develop the collections conceptually. We really made a strong, long-term commitment to fashion when we opened the Shenzhen studio in 2010. At the time it just seemed like the logical step to establish the studio in China.

It feels like ffiXXed enjoys exploring the cracks in the fashion system rather than rigidly following rules. Could you talk about how the brand operates? For us, ffiXXed is a framework through which to explore various aspects of everyday life, which of course is always changing and evolving. We're not necessarily opposed to the fashion system, but we have always been more interested in finding our own working models and rhythms. Since we never set out to start a fashion label it has been a very natural progression for us to work in this way. It has been good for us to question the way things are done and try to find new ways of working.

Your interpretation of the body exudes a unisex vision. What are the main differences when designing menswear and womenswear and how do these overlap? We began as a unisex label but have more recently focused on men's and women's collections separately. There is still an underlying unisex approach, and a lot of overlap between the men's and women's collections. Working with the men's collections we tend to start with basic shapes and there is a focus on subtler details and finishing. With the women's collections the silhouette is much more important. We start with proportions and shapes and work from there. There is a lot more movement within the women's collections so we can be a little more adventurous. But there are always certain styles that carry over from the men's to the women's and vice versa.

You are based between Hong Kong and Wutong Mountain, Shenzhen. What impact has this had on your design? When we first arrived in Wutong Mountain it felt a little bit like uncharted territory, and there was a great sense of freedom that came with that. Now there is more momentum, more things happening here, so it's very exciting and energizing to be a part of that. Living between Wutong Mountain and Hong Kong has really changed our approach to the idea of lifestyle, and this has had a big impact on the way we understand design, and what we want to produce creatively. ffiXXed is a very responsive project, so it changes as our own working and living situation changes.

Your clothing is produced in your mini factory in Shenzhen. What are the benefits of this? From the very beginning it was really important for us to be connected in a meaningful way to our production. We didn't feel comfortable

'ffiXXed is a framework through which to explore various aspects of everyday life'

outsourcing our production to unknown factories because of concerns about working conditions, as well as with quality control. After our second season we decided that we should establish our own production studio and it made sense to do this in Shenzhen since there was already a well-established infrastructure with access to resources and a highly skilled workforce, and it is still very connected to Hong Kong.

Your photoshoots look like fun. Did you work with a stylist to develop the look of the label or is it something that developed organically over time? The shoots are really fun to do! We often shoot in China around our studio in Wutong Mountain. The environment here is really interesting. The ffiXXed style is definitely something that has developed and evolved more organically. Generally, we do all styling and graphic work ourselves, but we often collaborate with other artists or designers, which informs different elements within the collection as well as the overall feel or style.

As recent finalists of the International Woolmark Prize you presented a collection in Milan (February 2014). Did you find you approached that collection differently, knowing that it would be the focus of such attention? We did take a very specific approach to that collection for Woolmark, mainly due to the criteria of the prize. There was a focus on innovation with wool fibre, but at the same time the collection had to be commercially viable with a kind of global appeal. So, we took a merino wool fibre as the starting point for the collection. The overall theme of the collection was related to domestic spaces, home furnishings,

comforts of the home but re-imagined through merino wool. We wanted to produce something that could sit alongside any other ffiXXed collection, but at the same time it needed to have its own identity. To be honest, we were so immersed in developing the collection we didn't really think about any of the press attention until we arrived in Milan for the show.

While your collections are stocked internationally, most of your stockists seem to be in Japan. Why do you think your design ethos resonates so strongly there? There's a certain approach to fashion in Japan that fits well with our brand. Our audience in Japan tends to be interested in the project as a whole, not just the fashion side of it. There is a lot of space there for things that are new and young and maybe a little more experimental, and a real appreciation of quality production and finer details.

Finally, where do you think you fit into the current climate of Chinese design? Stylistically or conceptually it's hard to say, as the landscape of fashion and design in general seems very broad in China at the moment. We tend to feel connected to people who are interested in building a more international community around design in China.

Page 82: Woolmark collection. 2014.
Opposite: AW13.

<u>Opposite and this page:</u> Looks from AW14.

GUO PEI

AN EARLY PIONEER OF THE CHINESE FASHION INDUSTRY, GUO PEI HAS BEEN WORKING WITH TEXTILES SINCE GRADUATING IN FASHION DESIGN IN 1986. SINCE 1997, HER ROSE STUDIO BRAND HAS BEEN PRODUCING FASHION FANTASIES REMARKABLE FOR THEIR INTRICATE EMBROIDERY, ELABORATE CUTS AND UNRIVALLED OPULENCE. REGULARLY DRESSING CHINESE CELEBRITIES, HER ANNUAL FASHION SHOWS AT CHINA FASHION WEEK ARE SPECTACLES THAT DRAW HEAVILY ON CHINESE HERITAGE.

Why did you decide to specialize in haute couture? I enjoyed fashion design even when I was quite young. It allowed me to realize and create beautiful things, and I knew it was the career that I wanted to devote myself to. When I graduated in 1986, I worked for a couple of different companies as a designer and received a lot of recognition, but designing for the ready-to-wear market bored me. I'm quite an emotional designer and I wanted to find a path that would allow me to express my particular take on glamour.

Could you talk about the standards of the couture system in China? There is no huge difference between how haute couture operates in China and France. Both couture associations demand the highest standards in craftsmanship, pattern cutting and personalized service within the fashion industry. In Asia, there is a very strict process that has to be followed and providing a one-to-one service to clients is key, with up to six different fittings. We work closely with the client to understand her specific needs and we base everything – patterns, fabric, colour – on those needs, from sketching out the initial designs to taking precise measurements and creating a garment that showcases the unique beauty of a client's body. Haute couture to me is not just cloth, but a dream, a history. It epitomizes art, wisdom and craftsmanship.

Does Chinese craftsmanship influence your techniques? From a young age, I was interested in and appreciated traditional craftsmanship. When I started designing, I felt that Chinese fashion was missing this connection to the past. It seemed a pity, so I began to integrate historical styles into my design, but without exaggerating them. I also made use of traditional skills and expertise.

Could you talk about why you choose to use particular Chinese symbols and motifs? As a Chinese designer, I do try to communicate my understanding of Chinese culture through fashion. Take my 'Story of the Dragon' collection as an example. In China, the dragon is a symbol of power and unobtainable beauty – just like haute couture, which is similarly beautiful but out of the reach of most people.

You designed costumes for the 2008 Beijing Olympics opening ceremony. What did that involve? I designed 280 different looks for the ceremony, a huge number. The embroidery, patterns and cuts all varied substantially, especially for the qipaos. The whole collection took more than a year to produce.

Finally, who is buying couture in China? I have many different types of customer. Their one unifying characteristic is that they are seeking premium quality and service, and a unique aesthetic. Initially, friends introduced my customers to me, but with the rise of the brand's reputation clients now include Chinese celebrities, businesswomen and even Peng Liyuan, wife of the party leader. I also have clients from the US, the Netherlands and the UK.

Opposite: 'The One Thousand and Second Night' collection, 2010.

'More and more people are
focusing on quality, the culture
and art behind fashion'

'Detailing and structure
are vital for me'

Models backstage, SS14.

HAIZHEN WANG

BORN IN CHINA'S NORTHEASTERN PORT CITY OF DALIAN, HAIZHEN WANG FOUNDED HIS WOMENSWEAR LABEL IN LONDON IN 2010. TWO YEARS LATER HIS STRONG TAILORING INFUSED WITH ARCHITECTURAL REFERENCES WON HIM THE CITY'S PRESTIGIOUS FASHION FRINGE AWARD. HIS SLEEK, WARRIOR-LIKE SILHOUETTES OFTEN PAIR MILITARY REFERENCES WITH DECONSTRUCTED DETAILS FOR A CONTEMPORARY AND ANDROGYNOUS LOOK. IT'S AN APPROACH THAT CLEARLY APPEALS TO HIS INTERNATIONAL AUDIENCE, WHICH IS GROWING YEAR ON YEAR.

Why do you think your designs stand out? My designs are not intended to warrant attention. I focus on what I want to do and put my best effort into it. If the resulting designs are successful and generate some interest, then it is their personality that has made the difference.

How did your fashion education in China compare with the teaching at Central Saint Martins? I would say I gained most of my technical and craftsmanship skills in China, whereas CSM helped me focus more on personal style and developing a sense of creativity.

While London is your base, have you ever been tempted to relocate to China? Not really, though I have been thinking about expanding my business into China, especially my hometown, Dalian.

Could you talk about your manufacturing process? I have kept production in the UK as it allows me to keep a close eye on the quality and progress. Additionally, I work with Italian manufacturers to source my materials.

How does your Chinese background underpin your brand? Besides its influence on my overall aesthetic, it explains my commitment to functionality, detailing and structure.

What role does jewelry play in your catwalk looks? I have been working with jewelry designer Maria Piana since AW13. My silver pieces were all designed by her and completed the looks while still matching my overall vision.

How do you deal with the pressures of the fashion cycle? It is a competitive industry and everyone has his or her own way of dealing with the pressure. I have learned to transform pressure into power and that pushes me forward.

<u>This page:</u> Catwalk look from AW13.
<u>Opposite:</u> Catwalk look from SS13.

<u>Opposite:</u> Catwalk looks from SS14.
<u>This page:</u> Catwalk looks from AW13.

HE YAN

HE YAN'S UNCONVENTIONAL APPROACH TO THE FASHION INDUSTRY MEANS THAT SHE OPERATES ALMOST EXCLUSIVELY OUTSIDE THE SEASONAL SYSTEM. SHE ALSO ONLY WORKS WITH CLIENTS WHOM SHE CONSIDERS FRIENDS. YET DESPITE THIS, HER TALENT AND NATURAL EYE FOR SIMPLE CUTS AND CLEAN LINES HAS ENSURED HER BREAKTHROUGH, RESULTING IN GARMENTS THAT ARE MUCH SOUGHT AFTER.

You were born into a family of tailors. Was fashion present when you were growing up? When I was young my mother did not allow me to use the sewing machine, because she didn't want me to be a tailor like her – she wanted me to have a more respectable occupation like a teacher. I didn't even learn basic sewing until I was at university as a fashion student.

When did you actually decide you wanted to be a designer? I never thought of becoming a fashion designer when I was younger, although I did enjoy drawing. I didn't know that there was such a profession until I went to university. Even after graduation, I was only passively involved in the fashion industry and would not have considered myself a fashion designer until the past two or three years, when I began to seriously ponder the value of my job to my surroundings and myself.

Could you talk about your vision as an independent designer? I began to design independently in 2004 and I did my first show only to realize my dream of seeing my designs shown as a collection. Consumers came to buy my designs and I realized that I could make a living from it, so I continued. Fashion for me is more like a means for self-expression instead of an occupation. I don't create a certain look intentionally and I don't promote a brand DNA (although those things do come into existence spontaneously to some extent). I don't even care about losing target customers – I only need to be loyal to myself and create the things that I think deserve to be shared.

What have been the main influences on your design aesthetic? In the early days my design was influenced by the work of designers I liked, such as Miuccia Prada and Yohji Yamamoto. Later I became interested in environmental protection, although this is an extremely complicated topic and I am still in the learning process.

How do you develop your client base? My client base is largely formed from my social network. I expand this network through doing shows, and there will be lots of potential partners and customers in the new acquaintances I make. I am not good at maintaining business relationships with people I can't get along with, which means that only the people I like have the chance to become my long-term customers.

You collaborate with the retailer Dong Liang. Could you talk about this relationship? When the two co-founders first approached me I didn't know anything about them. As I began to learn more, what really touched me was not their store or sales, but their sincerity. I decided to cooperate with them, and to my surprise my clothes have been popular in Dong Liang. They never interfere in my design and respect my way and pace of working. I think I am lucky.

What informs your practice and what do you want to express in your body of work? I try to incorporate anything I am interested in into my work; for example, I like modern dance, so I included this as part of my runway show. In every period of my life I will develop interest in certain things, and this is my method of working. I want to express my curiosity for the world. If there ever comes a day when I have nothing to express, I will just give up my design and creation.

Previous page: Catwalk, 2014.

This page: Looks from October, 2013.
Opposite: Dress, July 2012.

'I don't think my aesthetic represents Asia, and I don't even think it represents China. I think it only represents myself at the time'

HELEN LEE

HELEN LEE

THE CITY OF SHANGHAI IS INTEGRAL TO HELEN LEE AND HER DESIGNS PROUDLY STATE THIS
WITH THEIR 'MADE IN SHANGHAI' LABELS. HER FIRST LINE, INSH, WAS AN EXPERIMENT IN
STREETWEAR AND CASUALWEAR, HOWEVER, HER MOST RECENT BRAND DELIVERS FEMININITY
AND INNOVATION WITH STRONG GLOBAL APPEAL. WITH HER INTERNATIONAL OUTLOOK HELEN
LEE COULD WELL BE ONE OF CHINA'S NEXT BREAKTHROUGH DESIGNERS.

How has the landscape of the local industry changed since you started your first brand, Insh? When I started my Insh brand, people were more interested in casualwear. There were lots of brands around then that adopted a French- or Italian-sounding name, believing that anything that appeared to have been designed locally would be undesirable. I have always marketed my work as 'Made in Shanghai' and when we started I would say 80 per cent of our customers were international. That started to change with the arrival in China of popular TV shows such as *Sex and the City*, fashion magazines including *Elle* and *Vogue*, and microblogging site Weibo. These began to educate the local market and challenged people to seek out new ways of expressing themselves.

What made you decide to start designing under your name? Our customers started to ask for more sophisticated clothes and I wanted to start creating products that were more feminine, more fashionable and more creative. The brand is my dream, I am very driven. My small team of very focused people is an advantage as we can move faster and control the brand image well, and running our own stores is a crucial part of that.

You are a graduate of the International School of Fashion, Arts and Design in Montreal and now teach at Donghua University in Shanghai. What is your opinion of how fashion design is taught in China? Basic skills get taught very well in China, especially drawing. International schools teach creative thought differently and focus more on critical thinking. I think many students seek an international education for the experience of living in another country.

Did your experience in Japan mould your approach to design? In Japan I focused on textiles and there I learned about quality and the fundamental importance of great execution and originality.

Do you see any similarities between Chinese and Japanese design? I think that the trends in Japanese design are on simple details, while China right now is attracted to more expressive looks.

How do you consider your brand in relation to the wider context of contemporary Chinese fashion? We are a key player in innovative contemporary fashion. Helen Lee has been striving to keep doing things better, fresh and different from the start, which I believe gives us a lot of influence.

Could you talk about your sourcing of fabrics? Fabrics are fundamental to us, and we face the problem common to many small businesses of not being able to reach minimum order requirements. I take a lot of care to get the best fabrics, and we can add print dye in-house to make fabrics unique and personal to the brand.

How important have your shops and stockists been in building up your brand? Shops can be put together quickly in Shanghai and it's good to be able to start with something small and manageable. We choose our stockists carefully and we love it when they have a different approach and market as it helps to refresh our brand and reach new clients.

As one of the first Chinese designers to be stocked by luxury retailer Lane Crawford, how important do you think Chinese retailing support is in propelling the design industry? It's so great to have such a well-regarded retailer recognize what is happening in the Chinese fashion world. I know they truly believe that the designers they select belong in the same store as the international major players.

Your collaborations include projects with large, international brands like Dulux and Disney. Why are these companies attracted to Helen Lee? We get these opportunities because of our reputation for being a very creative brand with professional execution. These projects help us showcase our talent and our ability to be versatile.

Finally, would you ever consider relocating from Shanghai? As we grow we would love to have other locations, but we won't turn our back on Shanghai. The energy in this city and the response to our brand has all been so great. This city has given me so much and Shanghai will always be home for the Helen Lee brand.

This page and opposite: Looks from AW14.

<u>This page and opposite:</u> Looks from SS14.

'I wanted to build a contemporary
Chinese brand that could break
from the past'

HUISHAN ZHANG

RAISED IN THE EASTERN CHINESE CITY OF QINGDAO AND TRAINED AT CENTRAL SAINT MARTINS, THIS RISING STAR CREATES WOMENSWEAR THAT IS DIRECTIONAL YET UNDENIABLY FEMININE. WHILE STILL A STUDENT, HE WAS HANDPICKED BY DELPHINE ARNAULT TO WORK AT DIOR'S HAUTE COUTURE ATELIER. HE FOUNDED HIS EPONYMOUS LABEL IN 2010 AND QUICKLY ESTABLISHED AN ENVIABLE LIST OF INTERNATIONAL STOCKISTS.

It's an exciting time for Chinese fashion. How are you working to reinvent the phrase 'Made in China'? I deliberately want to create different associations for the label 'Made in China', which has become stereotyped. I want to highlight another view. Quality and craftsmanship have always been part of China's rich culture and heritage, so this is not something I am creating but I am going out of my way to shine a light on the beauty of 'Made in China' products.

Do you identify yourself as a Chinese designer? At the end of the day, you don't win people over with a geographical location or a garment label. What matters is the design, the pattern cutting, the fabric, and the way you communicate with the customer and your belief in what you're doing.

You have lived in New Zealand, France and the United Kingdom as well as China. Which country or experience has shaped your designs the most? My Chinese heritage is most important to me. It is part of what makes me the designer I am. I love bringing my culture to the West and bringing Western culture to the East, harmoniously bridging the two. The mix of China and the modern Western world is a part of my own experience so it is very natural for me to work with both influences. I see so much beauty in Chinese culture.

Where is your label based? My design studio is based in London but the atelier that houses our sampling and production work is based in my hometown of Qingdao. The combination works well and very naturally for me as both London and Qingdao feel like home and are part of my story as a designer.

How are your patterns constructed? Pattern cutting is vital in the design process and I love working with patterns and the craftsmanship involved. I take a couture approach, making the garments as seamless and light as possible. From the beginning, I have combined traditional Chinese design methods, using flat shapes of fabric on the body, with my Western pattern-cutting education.

How do you incorporate ancient traditions of Chinese mathematics into your design process? Using ancient Chinese mathematics to develop patterns came about very naturally while I was working with the smocking technique. To work out how to create seamless garments where the smocking travels right around the body I turned to traditional Chinese algebra, which uses interlocking triangles and trigonometry to solve equations.

The V&A in London acquired a dress from your first couture collection in 2010. What was the significance of this to you? This was a real moment of confirmation of my fashion career. At that time China was not yet on the fashion map, and this showed how open the museum is to new, non-established talent.

How did it feel to win the Dorchester Collection Fashion Prize in 2013? Winning the prize was amazing. It was great to have that international recognition. *Vogue* China has been supporting me since day one, and editor Angelica Cheung has particularly mentored and encouraged me. I share this award with her.

Page 108: Blue embroidered dress with Swarovski detail, SS14.
This page and previous spread: Couture collection, 2011.

'The ancient use of simple, 2D shapes
to solve complex, real-life questions
has a beautiful symmetry'

<u>Above left:</u> Mood board, SS14.
<u>Above right:</u> Illustration, SS14.

JNBY

SINCE OPENING IN 1994 WITH JUST TEN SEWING MACHINES, LIN LI HAS STEERED JNBY INTO A MULTINATIONAL BRAND WITH LOCATIONS WORLDWIDE AND OVER 130 STORES IN CHINA ALONE. THE BRAND'S NAME MEANS 'JUST NATURALLY BE YOURSELF' AND THIS ETHOS RUNS THROUGH ALL ITS PRODUCTS, WHICH FOCUS ON RELAXED AND DURABLE DESIGN. BASED IN CHINA'S TEXTILE CAPITAL, HANGZHOU, THE BRAND IS NOW A MARKET LEADER OFFERING WEARABLE AND DESIRABLE GARMENTS.

What is your brand ethos? Fun and passion.

Could you outline the working process at JNBY? Our year is divided into three seasons, namely spring/summer, autumn and winter. Each season's collection has three themes, some of which might be extended onwards into the following seasons. Usually the collection begins with what attracts or intrigues us the most. Our designers undertake research and then a mood board is produced, and at that point other design teams will join in and start to develop the work.

Generally speaking, how long does it take to produce each collection? Our SS15 collection, for example, took about five months in total, which includes three months of research. It cannot be considered 'fast' fashion.

How integral are your chosen materials to your brand identity? The fabrics and textiles we use are mainly developed and manufactured by domestic factories. The most representative fabrics of our brand are those made of natural materials.

Is it important to be recognized as a Chinese brand? Just as we have never underplayed or avoided this identity, it's also not something that we have been actively thinking about.

What are the advantages of basing the brand in Hangzhou? Hangzhou is where I grew up, and my family and friends have always been here. I love the natural environment and landscape here, as well as the food. Moreover, my team feels the same way, and we have never thought about leaving the city.

Could you talk about the ongoing expansion of the brand? Our menswear collection was developed in 2005 and childrenswear in 2009. The reasoning behind both of these was that we knew we could improve on what the market currently offered.

How do you successfully retain your international following? We simply insist on the things that we are passionate about, and there will always be a certain group of people who appreciate that.

Do you maintain a company archive? No, we don't at present. However, it was recently decided that outstanding pieces should be selected and archived for the purpose of training, enlightening and inspiring new members of the company.

What is your key to success? We work as a team and are constantly on the lookout for new possibilities.

Opposite: Vintage. SS14.

<u>Above left:</u> 'Reconstitution' collection, AW14.
<u>Above right:</u> 'Hermit' collection, AW14.

LA CHAMBRE MINIATURE

AIMING TO CHALLENGE AND REDEFINE WHAT THE WORLD PERCEIVES AS A CHINESE FASHION BRAND ARE HONG AND JAMES CHANG, THE TAIWANESE BROTHERS BEHIND LA CHAMBRE MINIATURE. FOUNDED IN 2011 AND BASED IN SHANGHAI, THIS BRAND HAS A STRONG INTERNATIONAL OUTLOOK. THEIR DESIGN IS CONSIDERED AND PROGRESSIVE, WITH CLEVER TAILORING AND INTRICATE CUTS. THERE SEEMS LITTLE DOUBT THAT THEY WILL SOON BE VYING FOR THE WORLD STAGE.

As brothers, how do you find running a label together, and what does fashion mean to you both? We both have our strengths in different fields. I [Hong] am responsible for the artistic aspect and James for the commercial part. Each of us has to contribute in order to accomplish the best for the brand. For us, fashion is an attitude and a belief. Fashion changes from time to time, but true beauty is timeless!

Hong, how does your design process work? I decide the direction and collection theme, then both of us do the research. I prefer to start with sketches to get the general feeling of a collection before going on to drape on the mannequin to get the right shape and proportions. As soon as that step is done, James and I discuss about details, fabrics and patterns.

Do you consider your Chinese heritage when you design for your brand? Yes. It can be quite a challenge though, as we have to redefine what Chinese fashion is about, and how it should be recognized in a global context! Is it a style representing the wealth of the nouveaux riches or emerging middle class? Or maybe a style that represents the traditional Chinese culture and its philosophy…? Maybe the answer is somewhere in between.

Has living outside China made you reconsider your concept of design? Living abroad was a great help to understand the Western ideal of beauty, its values and also the driving forces behind all this. There are so many elements to get inspired by throughout the world and its history. I [Hong] see them all as leaves of a tree that are kept together by the trunk.

How has working for British brands such as Alexander McQueen influenced your work? That was a great opportunity for me [Hong] to experience the different processes of the development of a collection. It was really exciting to see how Lee would transform his imagination into reality through draping, just like a performance artist, and how he developed the collection and also gave it the final touches as a stylist. Working within the team allowed me to see how he expressed himself freely through his work.

How does running a label in Shanghai compare to how a label operates in London? In general you do the same thing! There are pros and cons for both. London is further developed and more refined in terms of high fashion and is an incomparable source of inspiration. Shanghai on the other hand provides a ground with many resources that are yet to be explored.

How important are collaborations for the development of the brand, for example your recent collaboration with Kopenhagen Fur? The collaboration with Kopenhagen Fur was important for us. A new brand like ours needs professional support both in terms of know-how and resources. Because of the trust and support of Kopenhagen Fur we were able to explore the theme of the project freely, which was a great experience.

Do you plan to expand internationally? Sure. We'd love to see La Chambre Miniature abroad and not only within China.

Page 118: Coat from 'Kaleidoscope' collection, AW14.
This page and opposite: Sketches from SS14.

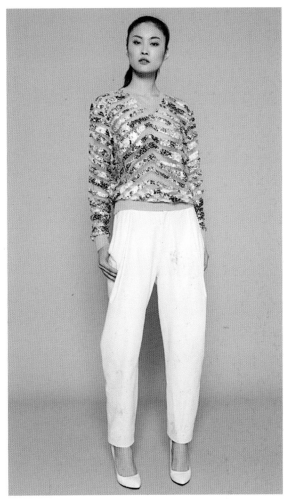

<u>Opposite:</u> Dress from 'Landscape' collection, AW13.
<u>This page:</u> Lookbook, AW13.

LAURENCE XU

AN APPRECIATION OF HIS COUNTRY'S RICH HERITAGE IS EVIDENT IN LAURENCE XU'S OPULENT AND INTRICATE DESIGNS THAT UTILIZE ARTISAN CRAFTS AND TRADITIONAL CHINESE SYMBOLISM. INVITED TO SHOW ON SCHEDULE AT COUTURE FASHION WEEK IN PARIS, THIS DESIGNER'S COLLECTIONS TAKE HIS TEAM MONTHS OF LABORIOUS WORK AND OFTEN INCORPORATE TECHNIQUES OF THE MING AND YANG DYNASTIES.

What are your thoughts on the fashion industry in China? Compared to other countries, the development of China's modern fashion design started relatively late. Chinese designers have the challenge of finding the design that truly belongs to China in the fashion world.

What drew you to fashion design? First of all, I love fashion design. Unlike other art forms, from the very beginning of the burst of inspiration to the final adjustments on the client, it gives me a sense of accomplishment. Without any exaggeration, I was born to be a fashion designer. I also carry a strong sense of purpose to promote the combination of Chinese and Western elements on the international stage.

What do you think are the most important attributes for a designer? It is difficult to learn design through textbooks without having your own experience. However, as a professional designer, one also needs a foundation in painting, along with historical and cultural knowledge and an appreciation of beauty.

When did you move to Europe and how did it affect your approach to design? In the late 1990s I began to tour and study in Europe. The experience gave me a more profound understanding of the differences between Eastern and Western aesthetics, but also the common ground they share. The differences result from their distinctive cultural spirits, and the commonality exists because of the same pursuit of beauty. I started thinking about how to combine the two in my design to show the world a brand-new perspective.

Chinese heritage is heavily referenced in your design. Could you talk about why you choose to revive these traditional aspects of Chinese design and how you are updating these for a new generation? Traditional Chinese handicrafts are undoubtedly artistic treasures, and in my design I combine them with modern aesthetics. For example, in traditional Chinese clothing the colours red and green are often placed together; however, in modern aesthetics, the combination of two strongly contrasting colours cannot be as widely used. Therefore, I apply these colours sparingly, using Western draping methods, to create a result that is both acceptable to modern aesthetics and reflects the unique culture passed down to us from ancient times.

Could you talk about your design team and how it works? There are around forty people in my team, divided into different groups such as design, pattern making, decoration, pattern and production.

How much work goes into the preparation of your catwalk shows? For a big show every small detail and seemingly insignificant choice entails great effort and requires significant commitment. The process of constantly being outside my comfort zone is the most challenging part of fashion shows for me. I feel pressure both from the world and myself.

How important are the models and styling for each show? The models not only need to interpret the beauty of clothing, but also need to evoke empathy and resonance with the garment to reinforce that beauty. The styling needs to

ensure the completeness of the look, and both the hairstyle and the accessories determine the character of the dress and the overall first impression.

Could you outline the process involved in creating a garment for a client? The process starts with communication. I gradually understand my client's character and intention through this process. For high-end couture, it is vital to know our clients' characters and hobbies, not just the measurements of their bodies. Only then can I begin my creative process. When the hand sketch is ready, my design team and I will introduce the concept of design, fabrics and craftsmanship to the client. Listening to the client's ideas helps to perfect the design sketches. After collecting the basic data of the client's body, we proceed to pattern making and create a prototype dress made with grey cloth. We will invite the client to try the prototype dress and make the size more accurate. Then we will further

introduce the craftsmanship involved in dressmaking, such as embroidery. Finally, the client will try on the finished dress, and the stunning effect will be rendered.

Museums are now starting to acquire your garments. How do you feel about this practice? When my works are collected by influential museums I feel a sense of recognition and excitement. This allows more people to get the chance to appreciate the precious dresses with their Chinese characteristics. However, I don't set out for honours such as this; my work is for the ultimate pursuit of beauty.

Page 124, this page and opposite: Catwalk looks from HCAW13.

MASHA MA

DESPITE ONLY LAUNCHING IN 2008, MASHA MA IS ALREADY ONE OF CHINA'S MOST ASSURED LABELS, WITH A STRONG SENSE OF IDENTITY. BASED BETWEEN PARIS AND SHANGHAI, THE HOUSE HAS RECENTLY STARTED OFFERING A DIFFUSION LINE, MA BY MA STUDIO. CUTTING NEW GROUND WITH EACH COLLECTION, MASHA MA HAS SHOWN AT PARIS FASHION WEEK AND WON A WEALTH OF AWARDS FOR HER INNOVATIVE AND PRECISE HAND.

What is your opinion of Chinese design? Chinese design today reveals not only inherited culture and techniques, but also breakthrough into the new era. It is not just expression and accumulation of symbols and details of Chinese characters such as the dragon and phoenix, but a spirit interpreted deeper within the collection. Chinese innovation and quality have caught the eye of the fashion industry worldwide. While I'm glad to be one of the strong voices of Chinese design, my aesthetic does extend beyond my Chinese identity.

Could you talk about your time spent at Central Saint Martins, London? My time at CSM was very inspiring. Professor Louise Wilson's sacrifice and perseverance in fashion are most impressive. She trained and treated you as a real designer, not just a student. She could make you feel like you knew nothing, but I also learnt so much from her.

You were the first designer chosen to take part in the CFDA/ _Vogue_ Fashion Fund China Exchange Program. What did you gain from this experience? It was a great experience to take part in this programme. I absorbed invaluable experience from the elite of the American fashion industry. By the end of the two-week journey, I had a keen insight into the fashion retail market by understanding the workings of merchandising, sales and e-commerce.

Your catwalk shows incorporate a striking use of styling and make-up. Why is it important to create an overall look? An overall look presents a solid brand image of who you are and what you are offering. The catwalk is a good stage to bravely express your attitude and ideas alongside innovative and mature collections from around the world.

Your AW14 collection features surgical face masks. What was the rationale behind this? We used the masks in the development process of the collection because we had different-fitting models, and to retain a consistent image of the work we asked models to wear the embroidered mask. It turns out the mask fitted the collection well so we used it on the runway.

How does Ma By Ma Studio differ from your main line? My diffusion line, Ma By Ma Studio, shows a more vivid image of young girls who have grown up in the era of multi-culture and the information explosion. It's a completely different line with a colourful palette and casual style, meeting the needs of the youth of this era.

What has been your proudest achievement to date? I'm the kind of person who focuses more on the next step towards the next achievement. From this perspective, the best is yet to come.

What projects do you have planned for the future? We now have our main line Masha Ma, diffusion line Ma By Ma Studio and also a third line Mamour. There will also be a menswear line in the future. There are ongoing projects with other brands to be launched later this year. I can't give information now, but these are new forms of collaborations and I'm very much looking forward to the outcome.

<u>Page 128, this page and opposite:</u> Ma By Ma Studio, SS14.

<u>Overleaf:</u> Masha Ma, AW14.

MS MIN

FROM THE AGE OF FOURTEEN, LIU MIN KNEW SHE WANTED TO BE A FASHION DESIGNER, AND HER COMMITMENT AND DRIVE HAVE NEVER FALTERED. RETURNING TO HER NATIVE CHINA AFTER STUDYING IN LONDON, SHE STARTED MS MIN IN THE COASTAL CITY OF XIAMEN. HER GENUINE EXCITEMENT FOR THE POSSIBILITIES IN CONTEMPORARY CHINESE FASHION HAS ENSURED THAT HER BRAND IS ALREADY MAKING QUITE A SPLASH.

As a graduate of the University of the Arts, London College of Fashion, what particular training do you think Chinese students are gaining in London? It was an honour to study in London. Chinese students in England are not unique; students travel from around the world to study their global fields of interest. I don't think it's any different to a foreign business student studying at Stanford, for example.

Did you find that your thought processes were different to your European classmates? I think all the students had their own feelings and fantasies and definitely brought something of their own cultures.

Does Chinese history inspire your take on fashion? I'm inspired by all Chinese history, which is vast and very rich. Currently I create a Chinese capsule collection every year. This began when I moved home after studying abroad and found that women who were following the tradition of new clothes for the New Year (the Spring Festival tradition) were opting for Western clothes. So, I created a collection using Chinese fabrics in modern shapes and traditional Chinese shapes, refabricated or looked at in a new way.

Having studied in London and shown at London Fashion Week would you consider basing your brand in London? I am Chinese and China is my home. China's current fashion climate definitely makes it a good platform for new design and support of local talent. Many look at China today as the wild, wild East. The fact that all eyes are on China does sort of add a heat to what's happening here.

You successfully transitioned from selling on Chinese internet phenomenon taobao.com to independent designer showing on schedule. Did perceptions of your label change during this time? The expectations of my customers didn't change, whether on taobao.com or at retail outlets. Perhaps the perceptions of the 'taobao snobs' have changed. But this is completely irrelevant to me as my focus is just on the challenge to be ready earlier and earlier.

Does your base in Xiamen have an effect on your approach to design? My decision to live and work in Xiamen is a lifestyle choice. The city does not have the resources, the bustle or the fashion communities of Beijing or Shanghai, but it's quiet here, I can hear myself think and I'm close to my family, and these things are important for me. I do travel quite a bit, and I think this helps keep me inspired.

Where do you source fabrics and what is your process for creating and producing prints? My fabrics are sourced globally from places such as Italy, France and China. I develop my own prints, which are mostly based on art. I love the expression of a print and what it can add to a collection or a mood. The articulation of the print, whether woven or printed, is based on the season and my particular feeling or mood.

Do you fit into the current wave of Chinese design? I definitely consider myself part of the current dialogue of design in China today. And that is very exciting!

<u>This page and opposite:</u> Looks from SS14.

'The fact that all eyes are on
China does sort of add a heat to
what's happening here'

NICOLE ZHANG

HAVING PREVIOUSLY WORKED FOR MAJOR BRANDS INCLUDING DIOR AND PRADA, NICOLE ZHANG IS NOW FOCUSING HER ENERGY ON DEVELOPING HER OWN BRAND. BASED IN SHANGHAI, SHE SPECIALIZES IN UNISEX GLAMOUR AND, DESPITE THE BRAND'S YOUNG AGE, IT IS FAST BECOMING SYNONYMOUS WITH CHIC, ELEGANT WOMENSWEAR.

Your background is in visual merchandising. How has this practical experience helped you run a fashion label? I became a visual merchandiser in 2002 right after I graduated from my fashion design major at Raffles Design Institute. I dreamt of having my own label, and ten years' work experience in luxury visual merchandising allowed me to gain an overview and complete vision of how to run a professional and international fashion business.

Is your aesthetic the result of your European working experience? It's not a conscious choice but it's who I really am. I was raised by very liberal parents and from a very young age I was intuitively creative. I would say childhood was a fundamental period for me as a designer. My own design aesthetic is for a very nice shape, simple and invisible detail and not overly dramatic design. My time in Europe working at international fashion houses was certainly precious to me, teaching me the real meaning of luxury and how it combines shape, fabric and function. I would say this experience took me from being a dreamer to a practitioner.

Who was your first stockist and how important was it to receive that initial support? Le Lutin was my first stockist and I felt very lucky to cooperate with them on a basis of mutual appreciation, respect and trust. It was a very important baby step for our studio.

As well as stockists, you sell directly to clients from your studio. Will you also adapt your work according to their needs? We do sell our products to our VIP customers directly by appointment. They are attracted by our design, fabric and colour selection. We will change the detail of the design depending on the needs of the individual customer, but we won't ever change the fundamental image of our brand for them.

Do you sketch or drape on the mannequin? I sketch all the time, even though I don't love drawing as I used to. I do also drape for small details on a live model or mannequin, depending on how I feel in that moment.

You develop unique details in your designs, such as signature pockets and pleating features. How important have these techniques been in building your brand identity? The Nicole Zhang brand tries to deliver a perfect minimalist cut, but at the same time offers more than initially meets the eye. The fun details, the new fabrics and after-treatment techniques are a very important part of our identity, allowing us to surprise beneath the minimalist design.

What is the importance of colour in your collections? As an Asian designer, I understand how picky Asian customers are about colour choice in relation to our natural skin tone. That is why I custom-make my own colours for each collection. Our customers are thrilled when they see the skin-brightening results of wearing colours that have been specifically chosen.

What brand language do you hope to build over the coming years? Raw, elegant, masculine, contemporary, classic, effortless, sophisticated.

'What I love is a very nice shape with simple and invisible design detail'

This page and opposite:
Catwalk, AW14.

POESIA BY CHRIS CHANG

ORIGINALLY SPECIALIZING IN LUXURY CHILDRENSWEAR, CHRIS CHANG SOON REALIZED THERE WAS A MARKET FOR HER UNIQUE DESIGNS IN WOMENSWEAR TOO. HER MAXIMALIST AESTHETIC IS MAKING QUITE A STATEMENT ON THE CATWALKS OF SHANGHAI FASHION WEEK, WHILE HER PLANS FOR EXPANSION WILL FOLLOW ONCE SHE PERFECTS THE DOMESTIC MARKET.

You have a very vibrant and recognizable aesthetic, it almost feels like you are an extension of the brand. Would you agree? I wouldn't say I am an extension of Poesia, because I am Poesia, Poesia is me and all that I advocate in dressing. I design what I envision women should wear and what I want to wear. But most importantly, clothing is a form of tangible, everyday art to me, which communicates to the world the inner woman: happy, glamorous, spunky, energetic, whimsical, capricious, adventurous and dynamic. I think the combination and explosion of colours and patterns together are the most logical way to convey that message about the inner woman.

How important are fabric prints in your collections? Prints are the starting point of my collections, but I wasn't always able to find many to my liking, so I started creating my own prints. I begin with a collection theme, then the theme gets turned into interpretation of prints and the prints inspire the silhouette, it's all intertwined. But it always starts with a theme, for example 'Entomology' for AW12 or 'Fantasia' for SS11.

Do you employ any new technologies or innovative processes when sourcing your fabrics? It's difficult for independent Chinese designers to lead in the breakthrough of fabric technology. European countries are way ahead of China in coming up with innovative fabric composition. New fabrics are great when available to us in China, but it's not an integral part of my design. It's impossible to get factories to invent anything if there is no large quantity of order backing the time spent on research.

You have spoken of your interest in extremes and colour. How does this influence your design process? What can seem odd to most people is logical to me. I don't deliberately set out to find contrasts, I just use whatever seems natural to me, which often ends up being extremely contrasting and surprising to others. A combination of themes and inspirations will happen at the same time for me, and I put them together because it feels logical and natural.

Do you think your experience as a general manager at Prada has helped you to structure and run your business? The Prada experience has definitely helped me in many ways. It gave me credibility within fashion circles. It taught me the importance of a strong product, which is the core of any brand, and the importance of a whole business structure to promote that product. However, there is actually very little management experience from Prada that I can apply to running my own company in China. It's very different working with the Chinese compared to the Taiwanese and Italians.

Your catwalk looks are very carefully composed and constructed. Do you work with a stylist? I don't work with stylists. I have the image in my head of how each item will be styled when I design a collection. Each collection is designed with a very specific look in mind so there is no follow-up work on styling after the collection is completed.

You have been based in Shanghai since 2007. How has the fashion industry developed since then? The fashion industry in China has transformed and matured a lot in the

seven years I've been here. I think tastes are slowly maturing and there is less blind consumption for the purpose of display of wealth. There is more educated buying as more style information becomes available. There is now a bigger market for Chinese designer brands and this sector of the market will get even bigger as consumer taste level matures even more. There have been changes on the production side of the industry too, and what used to be a factory-intensive country now begins to offer design to the rest of the world instead. The cost of labour has increased so much that price is no longer the primary incentive for clients to produce in China. Factories now need to present added value by offering available designs. This opens up work opportunities for Chinese designers to work with factories rather than just for their own brand.

Given your origins as a childrenswear designer, where do you situate your brand within the wider industry?

I started with childrenswear strategically because I felt it was an easier way to break into the international market. My line of childrenswear with the theme of shrunken womenswear was an instant hit with Barney's New York and I got my first order from them in the first season of Poesia Children in 2006. I see my aesthetic translated into all sorts of products: homeware, menswear, shoes, bags, and the full line of products within fashion and lifestyle.

Do you have plans to expand internationally? Of course, with the time and right partner. I do believe we have to be good in our own home and own turf first before we can think about the world.

Page 146: SS11.
This page: Catwalk looks. SS14.
Opposite: Lobster dress. SS13.

Opposite: Dresses from SS14.
Above: Backstage, SS14.
Right: Showroom.

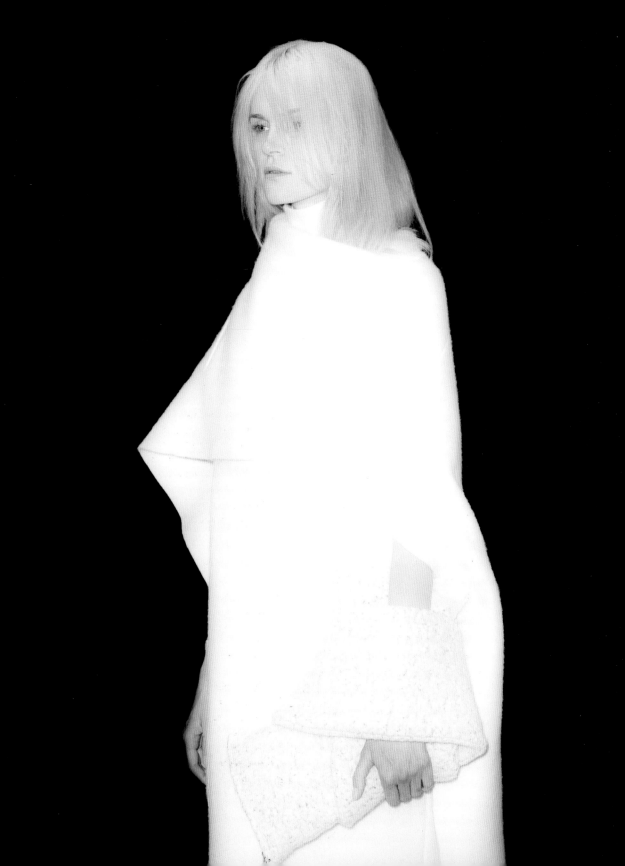

QIU HAO

FOR A NUMBER OF YEARS, QIU HAO'S DEFT HAND HAS BEEN RECONSTRUCTING THE VERY ESSENCE OF CHINESE FASHION, FROM THE SILHOUETTE TO FABRICATION. HIS PRECISE TREATMENT OF THE BODY, INSPIRED BY HIS ARCHITECTURAL LEANINGS, PRODUCES SWEEPING, LEAN SHAPES THAT PUSH THE NATURAL LIMITS OF THE FRAME. HIS INNOVATIVE USE OF MATERIALS WON HIM THE COVETED INTERNATIONAL WOOLMARK PRIZE IN 2008.

Why did you choose fashion as your medium? I started cutting and making clothes while I was studying interior and spatial design at college. At that time I thought it was an easy way to express myself. While making clothes you have to think of function first, while art gives you much more purity of expression. For me, combining fashion and art is the fundamental principle behind Qiu Hao. After that everything happens naturally.

Did you always plan to start your brand in China? Of course, I always wanted to go back to China. My family and my friends are all here. Life is always more important than fashion.

What are your thoughts on style in China? An individual's personal style is based on their cultural background and their daily life. Daily life in modern China has such a bias towards Western culture: what we wear, what we eat, what we drink, even what we desire. Meanwhile, there are 5,000 years of Chinese civilization trying to be heard. As a result, style in China is mixed-up and confused.

Why is being independent so important for your brand? To be independent is good for my creative side. It's purer to design something that follows your own desires rather than what other people demand of you.

How would you describe your approach to design? Every season my team and I spend lots of time searching for different ways to use a commonplace material. I like a minimalist style using different materials and a high standard of finish.

I am also very interested in detailing as I think this gives our garments a luxury quality. For our SS14 collection there were five different factories involved in the processes to create and finish just one skirt design.

You won the International Woolmark Prize in 2008. How did you cope with the press attention and interest? Winning Woolmark was a great experience, but I did not let it change the way I worked. I just kept a low profile and went back to my tiny studio to continue my design work.

As your brand expands, how do you maintain the quality and handmade finish of your product? We work with the best manufacturer in China who also works with many luxury brands. I do believe we can produce good design of a high quality here in China.

What are your thoughts on catwalk presentations in China? Catwalk shows allow clothes to be presented with movement, light and music. They are a good way to present a collection, but they are not the only method. Every designer can find the best way to showcase their style.

Do you think designers should always strive to create something new and constantly push boundaries? Fashion is not art. Fashion should be saleable. It is getting harder for designers to create something new. In fact, nothing is new. Designers can try to bring a fresh take on a familiar idea or materials, but achieving something completely new is no longer possible.

Page 152: Backstage. AW14.

This page and opposite: AW13.

'To talk about modern
Chinese style, we first
need to find out what is
modern China'

RANFAN

RANFAN IS DETERMINED TO PLAY BY HER OWN FASHION RULES. AS AN INDEPENDENT DESIGNER HER STRONG AESTHETIC EXPLORING GEOMETRIC DESIGN UTILIZES TECHNIQUES SUCH AS LASER CUTTING TO CREATE TRULY UNIQUE GARMENTS. DESPITE NUMEROUS INDUSTRY AWARDS AND ACCOLADES, RANFAN CHOSE TO FOCUS ON BUILDING UP A LOYAL FAN BASE BEFORE SHOWING AT CHINA FASHION WEEK.

How has Beijing changed since you first began working as a designer? The fashion landscape of Beijing has changed dramatically in recent years. A few years ago you could only find high-end luxury brands in Beijing. Then a wave of international designer stores began to crop up in the shopping district of Sanlitun and later the Lafayette store reopened and brought Beijing numerous foreign brands that were previously little known by the Chinese.

Is it important for designers to experiment? A real designer should make incessant breakthroughs, and constantly challenge himself. He can't stay in his comfort zone and repeat the same job for the rest of his life. Our SS14 collection took its inspiration from a series of images in my head, and at first they were vague and abstract. After two months' research, the abstract concepts became more grounded, and making them into reality has allowed me to experiment with new techniques.

Where do you source your materials? The materials we use come from various countries such as France, Italy, Korea and China. Any technical work with these materials is undertaken domestically.

Could you talk about the techniques you employ in your process, such as laser cutting? Back in 2007, I used a laser to make a pair of semi-hollow cut gloves, and I loved the unique result. Laser cutting has since become our most used technique, and although it is not 'new', heavily applying it in mass-production as we plan to do is still relatively rare. Our SS14 collection took its overall inspiration from this technique, with its central theme of light. I liked the idea of only using light itself to produce clothes.

You have won a number of awards in China, including Best Fashion Designer Award 2011. How important have these accolades been to you? These awards represent the industry's recognition of my work so far, and encourage me to continue with what I am doing, but to be honest, most of the time I forget about them.

Your brand has been in existence for a number of years now. Why did you wait so long to present a catwalk show? Even a few years ago the market was very immature. Fashion Week used to be a stage solely for a few major domestic fashion companies, and had little to do with independent designers. The market has leapt forward rapidly since the Mercedes-Benz China Fashion Week in 2012, which provided independent designers with a wonderful platform. This gave me the confidence to do my own show.

How does the fashion industry in China compare to other countries? China's fashion industry is young and energetic, and it has huge potential and room to grow. But China, as the world's factory, does not support or understand its domestic designers. Compared to other countries, the Chinese government could do more to support designers.

What would you like to achieve over the coming years? I hope the brand will mature and more people discover and come to love our brand.

<u>Page 159:</u> Campaign, SS14.
<u>This page and opposite:</u> Catwalk looks from SS14.

<u>This page and opposite:</u> Backstage, SS14.

RENLI SU

THIS PROMISING DESIGNER'S FOCUS ON MATERIALITY AND COMBINATIONS OF TEXTURES IS ALREADY GAINING NOTABLE ATTENTION. AS A GRADUATE OF BOTH THE CENTRAL ACADEMY OF FINE ARTS (CAFA) IN BEIJING AND LONDON COLLEGE OF FASHION, RENLI SU FUSES A COMBINATION OF CULTURES INTO HER HIGHLY DISTINCTIVE YET WEARABLE DESIGNS. WITH A FOCUS ON SUSTAINABILITY, THIS BRAND ALSO BOLDLY CHALLENGES THE NOTION OF 'FAST FASHION'.

What are your earliest memories of being aware of the power of textiles and fashion? It was 2006 when I first started at the Central Academy of Fine Arts, China, where I studied a variety of materials. Initially I did a lot of studying and systematic training in making patterns and the recycling and reconstruction of materials. I explored and searched for materials that weren't solely used for garment production. I became fascinated by vintage garments, especially very exquisite and crafty ones, from places like museums and markets.

Was your MA in Fashion Design Technology Womenswear a positive experience? Yes, it was definitely positive. My BA was also in Womenswear and as a female designer I'm more used to designing women's clothing. My MA allowed me to explore the topics of fashion that particularly interested me, such as history, ethnicity and natural fibres. The research I undertook during my study still serves me well today.

Visually, you mix many cultures, genres and eras. Why is this? I've always valued and admired ancient and ethnic clothing. Antiques from different cultures are also a great source of inspiration for me. But I do want my designs to be more customer-friendly and to not turn into costumes. By combining the ancient with modern fabrics and designs, I desire to introduce different cultures and histories to the audience.

Does any particular period of Chinese history inform your design outlook? I have mainly focused on the Tibetan nomads as a source of inspiration in previous designs. I'm intrigued by the lifestyle of people living in the Himalayan region, and what they wear now.

Your focus on organic and naturally produced material such as linen and cotton provides an alternative for the consumer. What inspired you to promote an awareness of responsible consumerism? It's because I'm tired of fast fashion, people getting rid of clothing season after season due to changing trends and low-quality, mass-manufactured garments. It results in a lot of unnecessary waste. I aim to preserve traditional handcrafted techniques and to apply natural and organic fabrics in my design. I think that Chinese customers nowadays are more open to ideas and have the willingness to find out more about a product.

Is your label an extension of your lifestyle and your thoughts about the current environmental situation? Yes, it is. I personally prefer a much simpler and quiet lifestyle and I think my label reflects that.

What designers or artists have inspired your aesthetic? I'm influenced mostly by the aesthetic of wabi-sabi, and the history of fashion. I'm also inspired by nature and artists such Mira Schendel, as well as works from documentary photographers. I like something that's real, not fairy tales.

Your lookbooks recreate very beautiful scenes, like tableaux. What inspires these? They are based on discussion with the photographer and the set designer. We talk about inspiration and the materials we use for the collection, and the

aesthetic of a particular few images that appeal to me. It's all about finding the right team to work with and so far I've been very fortunate.

It feels like a very exciting time to be an emerging Chinese designer. Do you feel any sense of pressure or expectation? It's really positive that Chinese designers are getting a lot of spotlight these days. Despite the fact that we share a similar ethnic background and a lot of us were educated in the West, the ideas behind our works are all different. This does come with pressure, however, particularly in sales and promotion, as the market we are targeting is rather niche.

What does the future hold for Renli Su? We will keep working to create and produce organic, austere, textural yet practical garments. We have also started to develop our own handmade fabrics. Undoubtedly it is going to be a long journey and it is going to take time to achieve our goals. We hope what we are doing can reach out to a much wider group of audiences who come to appreciate our collections.

This page: Dress, AW14.

<u>Opposite:</u> 'The Inability of Human to Stay Still' collection, AW13.
<u>Above left:</u> AW14.
<u>Above right:</u> 'The Tranquility of the Working Class' collection, SS14.

RICOSTRU

GUANGZHOU-BASED BRAND RICOSTRU IS WARY OF BEING SWEPT UP IN CHINA'S RAPID PROGRESS AND INSTEAD ADVOCATES A SLOW YET STEADY APPROACH TO THE FASHION INDUSTRY. FOUNDED BY MANCHIT AU, THE BRAND IS BASED ON THE CONCEPT OF RECONSTRUCTION. ITS CRISP, ELEGANT GARMENTS, WITH A FOCUS ON MINIMAL TAILORING, ARE ALL PROUDLY MADE IN CHINA.

You studied fashion design at the Istituto Marangoni in Milan. How inspiring was this time in Italy for you? My life in Italy gave me a lot of inspiration. Italy's delicate techniques, focus on quality, attention to cultural infiltration, and emphasis on classics and heritage; those are all the things worth learning. My education there allowed me to explore what kind of designer I was and what my aesthetic preferences were, and also taught me about how the commercially successful Italian brands operated.

Large numbers of Chinese students are currently studying fashion abroad. Do you see this as a positive step for fashion in China generally? Yes, I think this has brought about some positive changes, such as brand awareness, the requirements for quality, the control of visual elements, and marketing techniques.

How does Guangzhou compare to the more established fashion industries in Shanghai or Beijing and how does it inspire you? I chose Guangzhou mainly because the area has a mature clothes production system and resources, which was attractive for me as a designer without any base. A designer's inspiration does in part come from the city he or she lives in, but also from readings, listening to others and travelling.

Despite the size and population of China, the fashion industry is very small. Do you feel a sense of community between fashion designers and brands? As I choose not to live in the cities with heavy fashion atmospheres like Beijing or Shanghai I haven't really experienced in-depth communication with the 'fashion community'. However, I have to admit that as a designer who often travels to those cities, I can see sparks generated when I meet with the excellent fashion designers or other people in the fashion circle. However, this communication touches only a relatively superficial level, and I don't yet feel a very strong sense of belonging to a community.

How do your collections allow you to comment on Chinese culture? I think everyone now is focused on topics like 'East meets the West', however, for me, I don't intentionally apply Chinese elements. I believe that a person with real oriental spirit needs years of consistent self-training and cultural immersion, plus the gift to understand the culture. Currently my work has an overall direction, which is to use a modern aesthetic and materials to render the oriental spirit in my soul. I utilize my in-depth 'comprehension' of the culture, instead of solely applying the Chinese visual elements.

Ricostru is often cited as sustainable. How exactly do you engage with sustainability? To me, sustainability has many aspects. Firstly, most fabrics we use are environmentally friendly and this has been our focus from the first season. Secondly, we believe that a solid base determines whether a brand can succeed in the future, and creating classics that cannot be copied is very challenging for a brand. So, we slow our pace in our study of the material, technique, completeness and brand promotion, and we believe there is no need to rush. Lastly, 'sustainability' entails creativity and constant breakthrough, which requires us to broaden our horizons.

<u>Previous page:</u> SS14.

<u>How do you balance Ricostru with your other line,</u> <u>Manchit Au?</u> Ricostru is currently the major focus of our team. As the founder and core of the brand, I try to cooperate with the rest of the team to run the daily operation and creative process. We strive to reflect the modern pursuit of quality and an independent and young way of living through futuristic visual elements. The Manchit Au line currently only has high-end haute couture, and does not have ready-to-wear collections. I hope to develop it further in future when I have more experience in product design, and a better understanding of what I want the line to be.

<u>What do you think is unique about the Chinese client</u> <u>and how does this relationship work for you?</u> I think it is very important for a brand to have real empathy with its customers. It is an essential step for us to build a deeper level of communication with our customers beyond visual, sensual (trying on and feeling the clothes), and oral communication.

Ricostru's target customers are young individuals who have certain tastes and standards; they give attention to the quality and detail of clothes, love anecdotes in their lives and have an independent understanding of fashion. I am not excessively submissive to customer requests in my design. Rather, I try to guide them to get to know, understand and then digest our style and brand concepts.

<u>Finally, what challenges face a brand in China that</u> <u>advocates 'responsible' production?</u> In my opinion, the concept is facing great challenges because China is too 'fast': fast updates, fast fashion, fast information and fast changes in people's consuming habit. Many brands have to switch their concepts rapidly due to those market factors; and this is the major reason why a brand may lose its core DNA. The 'sustainability' we promote is a more relaxing and flexible way of living and working: to slow down your pace to feel the quality of things around you.

Opposite: AW13.
This page: SS13.

This page and opposite:
Catwalk, AW14.

RYAN LO

RYAN LO BURST ONTO THE FASHION SCENE IN LONDON TO GREAT ACCLAIM, WINNING SPONSORSHIP FROM LONDON'S PRESTIGIOUS SUPPORT PLATFORMS, FASHION EAST AND THE BRITISH FASHION COUNCIL'S NEWGEN. A GRADUATE OF LONDON COLLEGE OF FASHION, HE HONED HIS KNITTING SKILLS BY WATCHING ONLINE TUTORIALS. HIS SELF-PROCLAIMED PASSION FOR FASHION PRODUCES WOMENSWEAR THAT BLENDS FEMININITY WITH FUN.

What drew you to fashion design as a career path? I have no idea why but I just loved clothes, Blythe dolls and dressing up from a very young age. I am lucky my career happened really fast and spontaneously after I went to London College of Fashion to study Womenswear. I taught myself how to knit from watching online tutorial videos, as I wasn't studying knitwear in college. Then the Fashion East thing happened and now NEWGEN. But looking back, apart from the fun exciting 'hungry for fashion' juicy bits, I guess the fame drew me into the glamorous fashion world. Deep down maybe I want to be rich and famous. I want a different life, the wealthy, painless joyful lifestyles we see in magazines and on TV.

Could you talk about how you ended up in London at age sixteen and your relationship to the city now? When I finished high school in Hong Kong I had no idea what I wanted to do with my life. I loved shopping and clothes, so my mum practically filled out some fashion course applications for me. This resulted in offers from both London and Hong Kong, and as I had never been to Europe before I picked London. It was a quick, rational decision to come to the UK. Now I am here and London is great and is my home base. I am now established and know almost everyone in London fashion and they know me.

You have an incredibly fun and irreverent style. Would you say that running a label takes the fun out of fashion? It varies, but mostly yes it does take the fun out of fashion. It is a true test of my 'passion for fashion'. But then when things happen like Converse sponsoring you thirty pairs of free shoes and you happen to be a sample size, life isn't too bad! So it depends really on your angle.

What has winning NEWGEN enabled you to do that might otherwise not have been possible? They put me under the international spotlight and have brought so much attention to the brand from around the world. They helped us to put on our show during Fashion Week, which allowed us to showcase the collection, and they also give us business and showroom support. As we all know, fashion is a business after all and NEWGEN have helped me to turn my creativity and hobby into a real business.

You seem to have a wide range of influences. How do you define your aesthetic? The Ryan Lo girl is the perfect combination of sexy and cute. I stole that quote from the movie *Crazy, Stupid, Love* but I think in my case it fits beautifully. I love everything femme fatale, elegant and womanly, but also anything frilly, pretty, girly and almost princess-like. I guess I try to create 'character' clothing with personalities that women can relate to: whether inspired by the glamorous *Sex and the City* girls, the lonely Bridget Jones or the kitsch Hello Kitty. My wide range of influences comes from the fact that I have a lot of different interests. I think it's important to keep myself open-minded and try to feed the brain as much as possible. The world is huge and fashion is only a small part of it.

How does your Hong Kong heritage inspire your outlook? Hong Kong is great and it is my hometown. For me, Hong Kong is one the most diverse cities in the world. What

I do is mostly inspired from my childhood: what I loved and what I saw.

Your collections primarily feature occasionwear or 'dressing up' attire. What is the influence behind these looks? Growing up in Asia, we don't have many formal parties. So I love the formal occasions in the West: prom, debutante ball, the all-white summer in the Hamptons and 'ladies who lunch'. That's why we have the tweed suit, pussycat-bow blouse and the ankle-length jumper dresses as lounge wear. These items are perfect for the Ryan Lo girls to wear to have tea in Claridge's.

Where do you source your fabrics? When I first started my business I was a headless chicken. I would go to markets and source one-off fabrics, vintage buttons, the older the better. I only thought about the show and the final outcome. Now I can't do that anymore as I have an international business ahead of me.

How do you develop collections? Are they trend based? I actually think about trend all the time. Similar pieces to my jumper knits and floor-length knitwear can be seen in the collections of Marc Jacobs, Celine and The Row. Anyway, I usually work two seasons ahead. I am developing AW15 in my mind already. I like to be creative, playful and youthful. I am not here to do serious conceptual fashion, I am here to make girls and women beautiful and pretty.

What's next in store for the brand? In the short term I am looking forward to a lot of different collaborations, especially in accessories and jewelry. Long term I can see myself moving into areas such as cosmetics, cookies, home goods, cutesy childrenswear and stuffed-toy bags.

This page: Catwalk, SS14.
Opposite: Behind-the-scenes model polaroids, AW14.

Page 176: AW14.

ADWOA

ANASTASIA

KAIA

GRACE

SAVANNAH.

CHEYENNE

'Fashion is more than just
garments, it is a culture and
a lifestyle'

<u>This page:</u> Backstage polaroids, AW13.

This page: Catwalk. AW13.

SANKUANZ

FUJIAN NATIVE SHANGGUAN ZHE IS A GRADUATE IN VISUAL ARTS AND ADVERTISING, WHICH MIGHT EXPLAIN HIS UNORTHODOX APPROACH TO AESTHETICS. EMERGING AS ONE OF CHINA'S MOST FLAMBOYANT BRANDS ON THE CATWALK, HIS DISTINCTIVE TAKE ON FASHION IS HEIGHTENED BY CREATIVE COLLABORATIONS WITH THE ARTIST TIANZHUO CHEN. HIS WORK PROVES THAT MENSWEAR CAN EMBRACE THE AVANT-GARDE.

What made you want to be a fashion designer? Besides my passion for clothing, the real attraction for me was to set up a new brand. It allows me a way to promote my values and attitude. Clothes are an essential part of everyday life, so they are able to convey a certain ideology to consumers.

What is your unique take on design? I am interested in a lot of things, and those things are usually unrelated and even contradictory. So in my creative process, I frequently combine distinctive ideas and cultures together.

How do you translate your ideas into physical designs and garments? The starting point is an overall direction of what style and feeling the new collection will have. Drawing draft illustrations and choosing fabrics comes later, as the most important stage is the time spent thinking.

Could you talk about your collaboration with the artist Tianzhuo Chen? Tianzhuo Chen is a good friend of mine and we share a similar attitude and interests. We have been cooperating throughout all the Sankuanz collections and for the AW13 and AW14 collections he designed printing patterns and performing tools for use in our runway shows.

You operate from the city of Xiamen on the southeast coast. What are the benefits of this location? Xiamen is an island and a relatively isolated city. The downside of such a secluded environment for a designer is that there is less exposure to people and information, and it's not a particularly efficient working environment. However, the seclusion does provide an opportunity for independent thinking, allowing one to work and create peacefully without being distracted. Xiamen is also closer to production bases than Beijing or Shanghai.

Do you think Chinese men in general are open to unconventional fashion lines like yours? With the spread of the Internet, the internationalization of China and the rapid growth of the consumer market, Chinese male consumers (especially those born since the 1980s) have a considerable demand for unique fashion products. There is also now a greater general acceptance in society of avant-garde clothing.

Your presentations are fast becoming highlights of any show schedule. Do you work with a stylist for the catwalk? Styling is very important in creating the unique identity of a brand. I design all the models' looks myself in my runway shows. I think only I know exactly what I am trying to convey and the dramatic quality I wish to create.

What role do accessories play in your catwalk shows? We combine the use of accessories and other performance devices in our runway shows, such as the backpack. The backpack is actually a product in our collection, but the wood sculpture attached to it is a tool used only in performance.

The brand recently showed at London Collections: Men. Is international expansion a future plan? I hope to sell Sankuanz products in more areas of the world, to be discovered by more people and to bring our products into their lives.

This page, page 182 and opposite: Catwalk, London
Collections: Men, SS15.

This page and opposite: Catwalk, Shanghai, AW14.

SEAN SUEN

ONE OF CHINA'S MOST INNOVATIVE MENSWEAR BRANDS, SEAN SUEN IS PUSHING FASHION BOUNDARIES. NOT FOR THE FAINT-HEARTED, THIS BEIJING-BASED LABEL FETISHIZES THE CUT, COMBINING THIS WITH BESPOKE PRINTS TO PRODUCE COMPLEX SHAPES. WHEN THE TIME IS RIGHT, SEAN SUEN IS POISED TO MAKE A HUGE SPLASH ON THE INTERNATIONAL MENSWEAR SCENE.

Have you always been drawn to fashion design? I enjoyed drawing when I was young and I went on to study visual design at university. My first job was related to visual design and I fell in love with fashion design as soon as I got to know about the industry. It was then that I began to experiment and prepare to launch my own brand.

Where do you get the inspiration for your designs? I didn't receive a formal fashion design education, but what I learn from life and past experience will subconsciously influence my design for a season and become part of my design concept. When I design, I try to make the character of my clothes pop out.

How do your initial ideas progress to the end result? My team and I will try to materialize my initial ideas and inspiration. During this process there is a two-way communication with my team who will give me advice and feedback. It is a process of bouncing ideas off each other.

Prints often feature as a strong accent in your collections. How do you develop these? I design and create all my prints myself, and this is one of my hallmarks. This season my designs are based on the concept of 'emotions', and the inspiration comes from my thoughts about living in a city that is experiencing air pollution problems. The prints are derived from pictures of city skies; the little patch of grey sky that you see when you look up between the skyscrapers.

How do you combine the creative aspect with the more functional needs of running your label? Every year our company has a goal, and so far we have met these. Our company already has a complete operating system and jobs are divided into different areas such as design, operation, advertisement and production. Everyone has a specific job to do, and cooperation also plays an important part in the smooth running of the label.

Do you use Chinese male models on the catwalk? For the past two seasons our runway shows were in Beijing, and we used Chinese male models. However, we don't have a specific standard for the nationality of the models. We use any models so long as their styles are suitable for our brand.

Do you plan to grow internationally? Internationalization is an important step in making your brand visible on the world level, and we have been preparing this for a while. When the suitable opportunity emerges, we will take the step forward.

Would you be interested in working for another designer or house? If there's a good opportunity, sure.

Who is your ideal client? Those who love fashion and have their independent tastes.

Finally, what do you think of the current climate in menswear? The domestic market is not mature enough, but I believe it will improve. For us, this is a good thing. There are a variety of brands in the current market. The market will choose the winners and the better brands will survive.

Page 188: SS14.

Above left and opposite: AW13.
Above right: Coat, AW13.

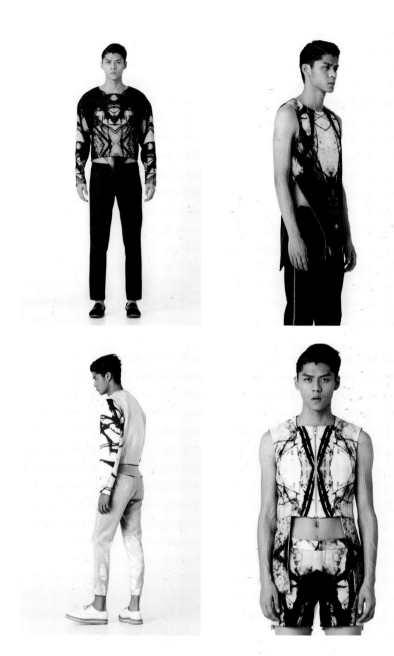

Opposite: 'Rebirth' collection, AW13.
This page: SS13.

SHANG XIA

BACKED BY THE FRENCH HOUSE HERMÈS, SHANG XIA IS ONE OF CHINA'S NEWEST LUXURY LIFESTYLE BRANDS. UNDER THE STEWARDSHIP OF CREATIVE DIRECTOR JIANG QIONG'ER, THE LABEL AIMS TO PROMOTE CHINESE CULTURES AND ARTISAN TECHNIQUES THROUGH ITS RANGE OF HIGH-END PRODUCTS. THE BESPOKE ITEMS IT CRAFTS HERALD A NEW ERA IN THE APPRECIATION OF CONTEMPORARY CHINESE DESIGN AND LUXURY.

What is your personal training and what drew you to Shang Xia? I [Jiang Qiong'er] was schooled in both Eastern and Western artistic traditions, which gave me the tools to create Shang Xia's design vocabulary. I trained in calligraphy and ink painting before going to study at art school in Paris. My mission is about more than resurrecting ancient Chinese crafts: our products must have relevance in contemporary China. If they don't have any contact with modern life, young people won't use them. It's the design that creates new life for the old crafts.

Could you outline some of the unique craftsmanship techniques that are being cultivated and revived by the brand's fashion line? Shang Xia is about excellent craftsmanship, contemporary design and very fine quality. It is the contemporary expression of a unique inheritance of 5,000 years of art and of living. Our recent cashmere coat, for example, was created by craftsmen who have taken at least fourteen years to master their skill. The coat features the highest-quality Mongolian cashmere and each garment is unique and sculpted into a seamless shape. The design is a contemporary expression of traditional Han dynasty clothing. It surpasses fashion and trend and is a timeless piece full of emotion.

Why is it important for Chinese culture that these traditions are revived? China has an image problem after years of mass-market, low-end and poor-quality production. But this view only relates to the China of the last twenty or thirty years. Looking back to the history of China, we have had the most glorious periods of Chinese arts and crafts, such as the Silk Road.

Even as little as 100 years ago, China had its own luxury brands: tailors, jewelry, shoes, tea and famous artisans. Then in the early 1990s the Western brand came about. This was fresh and new, so the attitude then was to put Chinese things aside. But more recently, some people have realized a need for their own cultural roots. Many Chinese people who come by our store tell us that our products make them proud to be Chinese.

The brand has a research team visiting villages, identifying techniques and documenting the results. Who exactly makes up your research team? The way Shang Xia preserves and revives traditional craftsmanship is different from what museums do. For museums, the main function is to record and to present back to the public. What Shang Xia does is to create a link between the old and new. We keep the spiritual beauty and excellence of crafts, and we add functionality to it, so that people can appreciate it, use it and enjoy it. In this way, the art of living happens every day in our life.

Does the company plan to train their own workforce in these techniques? It is a long-term task and we hope more and more people will join us. It is challenging to create an organic and continuously developing plan for the revival of traditional craftsmanship and atelier, but it is the right timing to start. A lot of younger craftsmen and designers are willing to join us.

How does the cultural remit of the brand sit alongside the business demands? Shang Xia is not a commercial project but a cultural one, although we truly believe that we

will be commercially successful if we focus on culture. We make an independent offering, rather than responding to what the market wants. We want to offer a cultural education and we believe the demand for this will develop.

How long does it take from concept to production?
The research and development time at Shang Xia is pretty long. Firstly we need to identify crafts, then the design team and craftsman need to sit down together to find the best way to translate the design. Finally, we test a product thousands of times to ensure it meets the highest standard of quality. The R&D process is continuous and we aim to bring more tremendous crafts into 21st-century life.

Do you feel your client base is mostly Chinese or international? We have clients all over the world. It is not just a brand for Chinese people or Western people. Our Paris boutique is the third worldwide boutique of Shang Xia, and the French people have been welcoming. I think that international customers are impressed by what's behind our brand: the modern China and the quality, creativity and power of culture it represents.

What can we look forward to from Shang Xia? We want to take enough time to do Shang Xia well. Time is essential to do things right. At this stage we are focusing on our core values: carrying the past to the future, pursuit of quality, cultural heritage and responsibilities.

Page 195: 'Lacquer' lacquered silk dress, 2012.
Opposite: 'Sculpture' cashmere felt overcoat, 2010.
This page: 'Carefree' cashmere top, 2010.

Above left: 'Clouds' cashmere overcoat, 2010.
Above right: 'Sculpture' cashmere felt scarf, 2012.
Right: 'Sculpture' cashmere felt vest and 'Clouds' cashmere dress, 2010/11.

This page: 'Jin Yi' quilted overcoat, 2012.

'What Shang Xia does through
contemporary design language is
create a link between the old
and the new'

'China is the fastest-growing global market
so it is very important to show here'

SIMONGAO

WESTERN DETAILING BUILT ON ASIAN SENSIBILITIES ARE THE TRADEMARKS OF THIS LABEL. AT THE AGE OF SEVENTEEN, SIMON GAO LEFT CHINA TO STUDY FASHION INTERNATIONALLY AND IS NOW WELL VERSED IN THE VARIOUS ASPECTS OF THE INDUSTRY. ALL HIS COLLECTIONS, WHETHER MENSWEAR, WOMENSWEAR OR COUTURE, SIT AT THE FOREFRONT OF A FASHION-FORWARD CHINA.

How did you become a fashion designer? I had previously worked as a fashion editor and fashion stylist, and these experiences made it a natural progression for me to become a designer.

How important is your Chinese identity to you? I left China at the age of seventeen to study overseas for four years. During that time I experienced different cultures, but I'm still a radical Chinese with a strong interest in Oriental culture.

Do you incorporate any traditional techniques or philosophies into your work? Yes. I use techniques such as embroidery and Zen philosophies, which I combined with urban chic in my last collection. I believe that heritage and reconstruction are good companions.

Does your Beijing base inspire your design? As the heart of Chinese culture, Beijing contains many different subcultures, and living here allows me to see how they all dress differently.

Do you experiment with any new technologies? Recently I have been doing a lot of work retexturing fabrics, which involved the application of new technologies. It is important to me that my work is fun in concept, but serious in product and well finished. I think that the use of new technologies to rework old standards is the sign of a good designer.

How vital is the fashion show? They are about building up the brand image. I choose what I want to present in the show, and then it's up to the audience how they respond to that.

Given your international experience, what is the draw to show in China? China is the fastest-growing global market so it is very important to show here. China Fashion Week is a well-organized event, and as a result of it Chinese customers are becoming more open to different brands.

This page, previous page and opposite:
Backstage and catwalk, AW14.

This page and opposite: Catwalk, London Fashion
Week, AW14.

UMA WANG

SHANGHAI-BASED UMA WANG LAUNCHED HER LABEL IN 2005 AND QUICKLY BECAME ONE OF CHINA'S FIRST DESIGNERS TO GAIN INTERNATIONAL RECOGNITION. THIS UNRIVALLED SUCCESS IS DUE TO HER CAREFULLY CRAFTED SILHOUETTES RENDERED IN SUMPTUOUS FABRICS. HER UNPARALLELED UNDERSTANDING OF FASHION IS TRANSFORMING THE REPUTATION AND POTENTIAL OF CHINESE DESIGN.

You have studied fashion both in mainland China and the UK. How do the academic and technical techniques differ? Both teaching methods have their advantages; in China fashion students are focused much more on technique, while in the UK there is a freedom that allows students to create.

Do you feel this combination of training is important to your brand's outlook and ultimately your success so far? Yes, it is. Like any building you need to have strong foundations.

You focus heavily on textures and surfaces. Is this core to understanding your aesthetic? For me, fabric is the fundamental element of my work and everything else has got to be built upon that.

You show on schedule in Milan, but what are the benefits of basing the label in China? China is the biggest market in the world, so it makes sense to be based there. I also have a lot of past experience working in China so I have strong connections with factories.

Why are Chinese consumers now more eager to support homegrown brands? People in China are becoming more independent. They are developing their own awareness and consciousness. They are willing to use their own judgment and recognize ability in the work of Chinese designers.

Why did you choose Milan Fashion Week to present your collections and what are the main benefits of showing on that schedule? The working system of the fashion show in Milan is very organized. It is also a great platform for me to show my work to the public, press and buyer at one time. Italy has also been one of the most important markets for us so far.

Do global consumers have a different interpretation of the body–garment relationship than your clients in China? Yes. Western people like to show off their body shape by wearing very tight clothing, whereas Eastern people are shy to do so due to our cultural background. In the East we prefer to be fully covered, as this is considered polite. It also makes people more curious about what is behind or underneath the garment.

Your collections draw upon a very neutral palette. Can you explain the importance of colour to your aesthetic? I don't think I am confident enough to use many colours. Neutral colours have a kind of purity in my imagination.

How would you feel about the display and styling of your work in fashion exhibitions? Good question, I've never thought about that.

'Fabric and texture are fundamental to my designs. Everything I do is built upon that foundation'

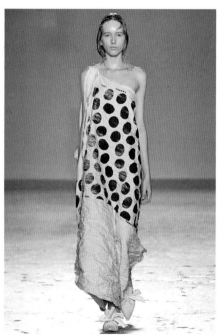

Page 206: AW12.
Page 209: Dress, SS12.

Opposite: Catwalk, Milan Fashion Week, SS14.
This page: Backstage, SS13.

VEGA ZAISHI WANG

EDUCATED IN LONDON, VEGA ZAISHI WANG NOW OPERATES HER EPONYMOUS LABEL FROM CHINA, PRODUCING ALL HER COLLECTIONS IN BEIJING. FOCUSING ON TAILORED SILHOUETTES WITH ELEGANT LINES, HER SINGLE-MINDED VISION ILLUSTRATES A SELF-ASSURED HAND. SHE IS ALREADY MAKING A NAME FOR HERSELF WITHIN THE CHINESE FASHION INDUSTRY, AND PROMISES MUCH MORE.

How would you describe the fashion industry in China? It is small, but it is also undergoing big changes. Since 2008 China has been opened up to the world. More and more Chinese designers who have overseas educational experiences are returning to China to set up their own businesses.

Your collection 'Alpha Lyrae' incorporated electro-luminescent technology. Why? Both my parents were engineers and I am always waiting for the next technological advance to allow me to push my work to the next stage.

How involved are you in the business side of things? As a designer I also have to take care of the business operations. Sometimes this is hard because design and business are so different, and that's when I draw on the expertise of my team. I still make sure that I give the overall direction and make the final decisions.

You run your label out of a traditional Chinese house in a *hutong*. Why did you choose to base your business there? *Hutongs* are a traditional type of narrow street or alley. China is a rapidly developing country, and many *hutongs* have been destroyed. I love *hutongs* because their unique environment represents the old city. They make me feel like I am in the 'real' Beijing, not just another city in China.

Would you say that you are a maverick of Chinese fashion? I don't believe that I will rewrite or challenge the rules of fashion in China, but I do want to show my feelings and how faithful I can be to my work and my creativity. I love to design because I feel free when I am doing it.

How important is Chinese culture to your work? I grew up in China and I am deeply influenced by the culture of my country. I bring elements of this into my design, through my clean cuts, classic feeling and uniform look.

Page 212 and previous spread: 'Unbroken LOULAN' collection,
AW13 campaign.

<u>This page and opposite:</u> 'In Love Again'.
SS14 lookbook.

XANDER ZHOU

XANDER ZHOU'S PRODIGIOUS RISE TO FAME IN CHINA SINGLES HIM OUT AS A LEADING EXAMPLE FOR MANY ASPIRING YOUNG DESIGNERS WORLDWIDE. HIS INNOVATIVE TAKE ON FASHION RESULTS IN MENSWEAR THAT PUSHES THE BOUNDARIES OF DESIGN AND CONSTRUCTION. HIS INSERTION OF CONTEMPORARY REFERENCES INTO HIS AVANT-GARDE DESIGNS MEANS HE FITS PERFECTLY INTO THE LONDON COLLECTIONS: MEN SCHEDULE WHERE HE CURRENTLY SHOWS.

How has the Chinese fashion landscape and its consumer changed since you started your label in 2007? Since 2007 China has seen the development of its own fashion scene, including a group of fashion consumers who truly appreciate original design and who are increasingly interested in domestic designers. Although this is a fairly recent development and the fashion scene is still relatively small, there are possibilities for new Chinese labels to establish themselves.

Why do you think there is such excitement around Chinese design right now? I think that China has caught the world's eye in recent years because of its rapid economic development and its increasingly noticeable presence. This attention does offer Chinese designers a certain edge. But I think it is important to remain realistic: the world is not especially interested in Chinese design, China just happens to be in the focus of the attention right now. I say we should grab the opportunity and make the best of it, but there are no guarantees.

China's fashion history is fascinating and complex. Does it influence how you approach the body or your design process? China has a rich cultural heritage. While I appreciate this, I have not (yet) found a natural connection between Chinese tradition and modern-day fashion in my own designs. Maybe I will some day, but certainly not by 'borrowing' traditional elements that are perceived as 'typically Chinese', because to me that feels too much like a 'scam'.

For you, what are the main differences between designers from Shanghai and Beijing? Despite its size and apparent diversity, China has reached a surprising degree of uniformity on a more fundamental level. Although geographically the distance between Beijing and Shanghai is greater than that between London and Milan, the two Chinese cities do not feel as far apart. To me, a perceivable difference is that Shanghai tends to be more business-oriented. Therefore, you tend to find more designers who have a stronger commercial presence on the Chinese market in Shanghai, whereas Beijing is a friendlier habitat that accommodates the kind of designer who enjoys living the life but does not have much to show for it.

As a menswear designer, what is your interpretation of masculinity? For me, there are two aspects of masculinity that exist at the same time and can be somewhat contradictory. One is the primitive, sex-appeal type of masculinity. The other is the masculinity that can be expressed through design. My intention is not to create androgynous looks or blur the line between the two sexes. I just tend to enlarge certain aspects of masculinity in my collections, but those aspects are not necessarily the ones that are stereotypically perceived as masculine.

How important is it to make a statement on the catwalk? This is of the utmost importance. There is quite a bit of homogeneity out there, so it is imperative to make a lasting impression. The most important criterion by which I judge my own collections is whether or not they are memorable.

You incorporate a variety of accessories into your presentations. How important is the complete look? The complete look is very important. There are several ways

'At the end of the day, it is the quality of your work that counts, and not where you're from'

to create a 'collection' out of a pile of clothes you make in any given season. It is about bringing order and coherence in the looks you send out on the catwalk. For me, the way is to let the collection breathe through every little detail, down to models, hairstyles and accessories.

Where do the majority of your sales come from and what is your most adventurous market? In London, my 'Boys Will Be Boys' collection sold out in one week. Sales in Hong Kong are also good. Perhaps mainland China remains the most adventurous market…

You show at London Collections: Mens. What makes you want to position your label there? Before London Collections: Men, I showed my collections in China (most often in Beijing, but also in Shanghai). LC:M came into existence at exactly the right time for me. Thanks to this fortunate timing and opportunity, London is now the place where I show my new collections to the world. And I have no reason to want to do it anywhere else. I like London, its freshness, creativity and promise of opportunities.

How do you make use of social and traditional media? Social and traditional media, such as magazines, are just other channels to express myself, like a fashion show. Through every channel you get to show a different side of yourself. They allow you to show people who you are and what you do other than designing. Social media is a two-way street: I share my impressions on Instagram, but I also see how like-minded friends look at the world. The 'Gay China' issue of *iLook* magazine, for which I was the guest editor, still stands as one of my proudest moments. As far as I'm aware, it was the first instance of a gay-themed issue of an officially published Chinese magazine.

What do you see for the future of fashion promotion? I believe fashion promotion in the future will inevitably involve multimedia and become increasingly interactive. I think that new technologies offer us exciting new ways to promote fashion.

Opposite: SS12.
This page: AW12.

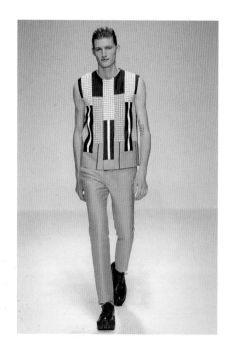

Above left and left: Catwalk, SS13.
Above: Catwalk, SS14.

This page: Catwalk, 'Mass Production' collection, AW07.

XIAO LI

GREAT THINGS HAVE BEEN PREDICTED FOR THIS CHINA-BORN, LONDON-BASED DESIGNER. SINCE HER ROYAL COLLEGE OF ART GRADUATE COLLECTION IN 2013 AND HER INTERNATIONAL TALENT SUPPORT AWARD, SHE HAS BEEN IN CONSTANT DEMAND WORLDWIDE. HER INSTINCTIVE EXPLORATION OF DESIGN PROCESSES RESULTS IN INNOVATIVE, VOLUMINOUS GARMENTS WHICH CHALLENGE THE LIMITS OF MATERIALITY AND WOMENSWEAR.

Your approach to design is unique and experimental, combining traditional processes with contemporary applications. Do you see it as the evolution of design? I think 'evolution' is too big a concept for me. But I always try to do something innovative, and I want to bring some fresh air to the fashion industry.

Does your Chinese heritage have any impact on your design? My personality has been built from a combination of my life experience mixed with Chinese and Western cultures. I try to keep my collection very personal, so Chinese culture does have some impact on my design. But my focus is to create something innovative. I also try to keep my brand international rather than specific to one culture.

Could you talk about your approach to the body and the fashion silhouette? I love sculptured and oversized garments. I just retouch classic garments with a modern fabric and sculptured shape details. I like to see people wear something different on the street.

Some of your garments are incredibly heavy, how wearable are your designs? I think it is important to differentiate between my show garments and those intended for daily wear. For my RCA collection there were many show pieces but there were also quite a few wearable items made using spacer fabric and cotton yarn. The capsule collection I just did with Diesel has much-improved wearability: for example, the weight of the silicon vest is no more than that of a normal leather jacket, and it is also safe for a washing machine.

Your AW14 final look included an illuminated jacket. Can we expect more use of new technologies in future? For AW14, I used LED lights because I want to move forward and explore something new in my collection. That LED silicon jacket was the first attempt, and there will be something more exciting in my next season.

You use a very restrained colour palette, focusing on pastel and whites. What is the significance of colour in your work? Colour always plays a very important role in my collections. It helps me tell the story of the collection and communicate with the people who wear the clothes.

Your fabrication is quite innovative, involving layering knitwear and silicon. How did this come about? The starting point of mixing silicon and knitwear was that I wanted to give people a new way to think about knitwear that was fun and surprising. I also like to play with new materials and silicon is one that I always wanted to try.

Do you ever design with the museum in mind? I don't yet. But I am open-minded about different types of collaboration and I would look forward to working in this way if there were a great concept or idea.

Finally, do you feel there is any sense of community or similarity among Chinese designers? I think that just the word 'Chinese' means that we have something fundamental in common.

This page and page 224: Graduate collection, Royal College of Art, 2013.

This page: Backstage and
catwalk. AW14.

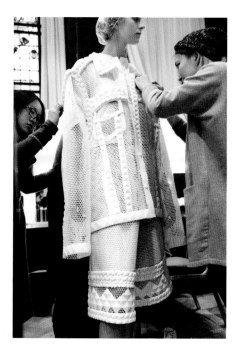

This page and opposite: AW14.

'I wanted to give people
a new way to think about
knitwear'

YIFANG WAN

INSPIRED BY ARCHITECTURE AND HER SURROUNDING ENVIRONMENT, YIFANG WAN USES A PROCESS OF TRIAL AND ERROR TO CONSTRUCT HER DISTINCTIVE GARMENTS. A GRADUATE OF CENTRAL SAINT MARTINS, WAN'S TECHNICAL PROWESS IS EVIDENCED IN HER DETAILED CONSTRUCTION AND CUTS, WHICH HAVE CREATED A NEW STANDARD IN WEARABILITY.

Why have you chosen London as your base? London is a very interesting and creative city. It is the perfect place to start up as a young designer. London Fashion Week drives me forward as there is a constant push year after year and continuous innovation made by the amazing people here.

Could you talk about your time at Central Saint Martins? The Fashion course director Louise Wilson was a driving force pushing me forward in my work. The environment of CSM is extremely creative and challenging. It really opened up my mind about art and design.

Your collections illustrate a love of draping and also pattern. Why are they such a vital component to your design approach? I am very precise so creating a pattern is creating a standard. Draping is a natural form and the idea of combining the standard of pattern and the free flowing of draping to achieve a kind of balance is key to my work.

Your self-made accessories are incredibly striking and sculptured. What is the craft process behind these? These pieces came about very naturally. I looked at sculpture and ways of combining different disciplines into fashion. I take inspiration from many things around me. The making of these sculpture pieces was very experimental. It was through trial and error that I constructed these and decided on the final shape.

What is the attraction of a retail space, especially considering the power of online consumerism? To me, it is about being able to express my feelings and my clothing in a choreographed and controlled environment. That way, when a customer comes into my store they understand the brand beyond just the clothing.

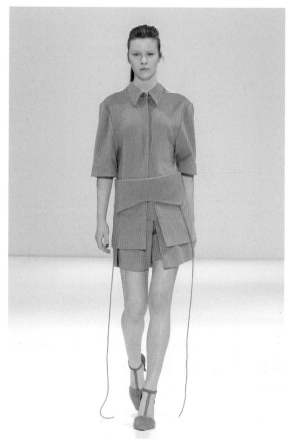

<u>This page and opposite:</u> Catwalk, AW14.

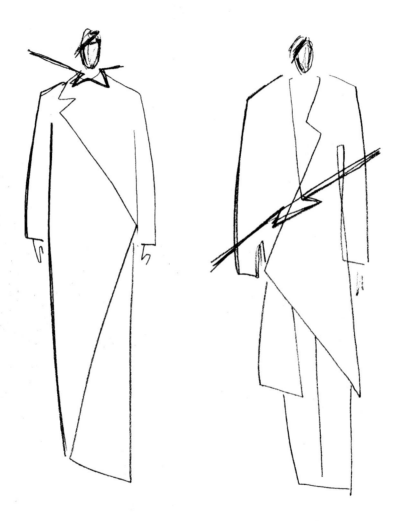

This page: Sketch from AW13.
Opposite: Dress from Graduate MA collection.

YIQING YIN

HAVING SPENT HER CHILDHOOD MOVING BETWEEN COUNTRIES, FASHION HAS PROVIDED A SOLID POINT OF REFERENCE AND EXPRESSION FOR THIS TALENTED DESIGNER. HER INTUITIVE DESIGN PHILOSOPHY CREATES GARMENTS THAT PROTECT THE BODY LIKE THE MOST LUXURIOUS ARMOUR. WINNER OF THE PRESTIGIOUS ANDAM AWARD IN 2011, SHE HAS BEEN SHOWING ON SCHEDULE AT HAUTE COUTURE FASHION WEEK IN PARIS SINCE AW12.

Could you talk about your childhood and your Chinese identity? I was born in Beijing but moved to Paris at the age of four, and then lived with my father in Australia from the age of fourteen to eighteen. My Chinese roots have been with me wherever I have moved and begun a new life. When I was younger people looked at me differently because China at that time was not the powerful market it is now. Since this incredible growth, I have noticed that people's attitude towards my origin has changed.

Would you say that your approach to design is a fusion of both Eastern and Western sensibilities? Yes, I think that my collections are a mix of Chinese subtlety and the legacy of French couture. But I consider the dominant feature of my work to be its simplicity, rather than Chinese or French influence.

Where did you train? I studied Fine Arts at the École Nationale Supérieure des Arts Décoratifs in Paris. I also attended classes at the London College of Fashion and the Chambre Syndicale de la Haute Couture.

What is your design process? I really care about every detail and I work in a very methodical way, step by step. I start by doing some research about inspiration and theme. Then I spend weeks analysing fabrics before deciding which ones will be included in the collection. When I actually start making a garment, I organize many fittings so I am sure it is wearable, comfortable, and that the movement of it is beautiful and smooth.

Where do you find inspiration for your collections? I'm mostly inspired by nature, such as the anatomy of the human body. I think the way the body is built and the architecture and structure of nature are impressive. This is the pure inspiration that I want to translate in my collections.

Why did you decide to focus on couture? I deeply admire the legacy of French couture, and I want to create a new vision of couture – one that is more modern and adapted to our generation and reinterprets traditional techniques based on pleating, draping and embroidery. It is a truly sensitive and instinctive approach to design.

Have you noticed any particular attributes unique to the couture client from China? Chinese couture clients are still conservative and tend to be more receptive to the big names and brands. However, they do also really like to discover new designers, especially those from France.

You collaborated with Bevilacqua for the 'Silk Map' exhibition at the Venice Biennale in 2013. How important is it for you to pursue creative projects such as this outside of the fashion system? I appreciate that art is not limited to couture and fashion design. Inspiration is everywhere and we need to stay open-minded and aware of the novelty all around us. Sculpture influences me a lot in my collections, particularly in the architectural conception of my clothes. Every single form of art has a role to play in the process of developing new sensibilities.

'I think that buyers in China have
a responsibility to promote less-
established designers'

<u>Opposite:</u> Catwalk looks from 'Les rives de lunacy' collection, Haute Couture Fashion Week, AW13.
<u>This page:</u> Ready-to-wear, AW14.
<u>Overleaf:</u> Catwalks, Haute Couture Fashion Week, AW11 and AW12.

YIRANTIAN

THIS AMBITIOUS YOUNG DESIGNER HAS SET HER SIGHTS ON RECONSTRUCTING THE FASHION FORM. HER UNIQUE METHOD OF THINKING ABOUT THE FASHION BODY IN TERMS OF STRUCTURE, SHAPE AND SCALE IS BREAKING NEW GROUND. A RECENT GRADUATE OF LONDON COLLEGE OF FASHION, SHE WAS PICKED UP BY CHINESE RETAIL STORE DONG LIANG WHILE STILL STUDYING AND NOW DIVIDES HER TIME BETWEEN THE UK AND CHINA.

Why did you decide to study in London as opposed to a university in China? Some of my favourite fashion designers are either from London or living in London, so I was naturally drawn to the place. Besides, London is a vibrant multicultural city, which is able to inspire me in many ways.

Did relocating to London make you reconsider your Chinese heritage? I have always appreciated Chinese culture and tradition, and I know that I am a product of it. Moving to London allowed me to value the Orient from a new perspective.

Could you outline your philosophical approach to design? In my design language, a simple design consists of many complex elements. A great diversity of design elements could appear on one single garment, and they work well.

Do you have a specific approach to colour? I tend to go for the bold colour and strong contrast, such as head-to-toe scarlet or black with white.

Do you ever cite architectural influences? Absolutely. Architecture has inspired me a lot in many ways, especially the structure of interior space, negative spaces, and the combination of lines and aspects.

How fluid is your design process? In my design process, redefining is a basic routine. I never start making the toile and sample until my concept has been fully considered and often reworked. I also always review and conclude my previous collections when they are complete. This whole process takes a lot of time and effort but it is really important for a collection.

Given that you trained in London, why did you decide to establish your brand in China? China is a much bigger market, which is developing day by day. Therefore, it seemed logical that I come back to start my career in my home country. I believe more and more international fashion designers will choose to come to China to explore the market.

How did you get selected to show at Shanghai Fashion Week? There is a fashion boutique in China called Dong Liang, which has stores in Shanghai and Beijing, and is a good platform for Chinese designers. They approached me when I was doing my MA, and they eventually ordered a mini collection of mine. With their support I was able to show at Shanghai Fashion Week for the first time this year.

How hard was it to establish production in China, given your small orders? I was introduced to my production company through a friend, as I didn't have any Chinese contacts after my time living in London. The factory is small, so the production cost is fairly high compared to others.

Do you have any mentors? In this industry, you get to meet many people along the way, and you get to learn more or less from any of them. Nevertheless, you have to make your own decisions.

What is the most important piece of advice you have received? Be who you are, and never stop exploring.

'In my design language, a simple
design consists of many complex
elements'

<u>Opposite and page 243:</u> AW14.
<u>This page:</u> Hand drawing of line-up. AW14.

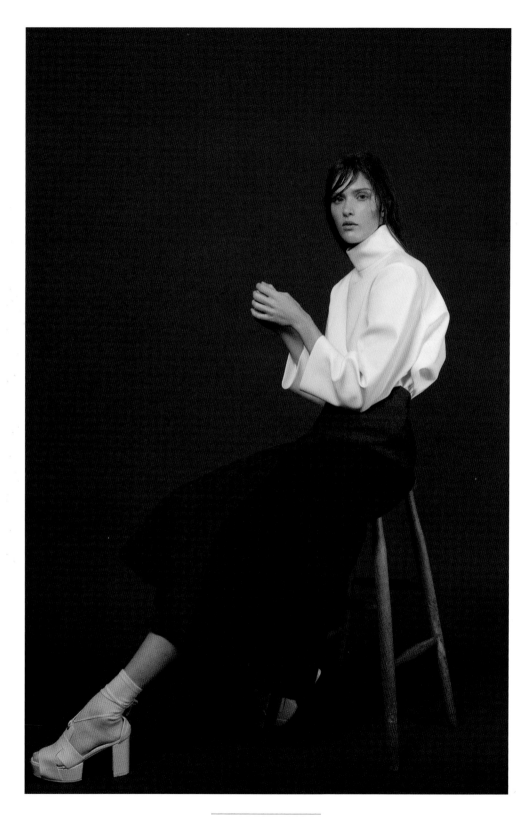

This page and opposite: AW14.

ZUCZUG/

OFFERING A NEW CONCEPT IN CHINESE DESIGN, ZUCZUG/ WAS ORIGINALLY STARTED BY ACCLAIMED DESIGNER WANG YIYANG OF THE BRAND CHA GANG. NOW, ALONG WITH A HANDPICKED AND DEDICATED DESIGN TEAM, ZUCZUG/ IS CARVING OUT ITS OWN NICHE WITHIN THE FASHION LANDSCAPE. OFFERING A FOCUSED BUT FUN AESTHETIC, THIS BRAND CATERS FOR ALL SECTORS OF CHINESE SOCIETY.

What is the design philosophy behind the brand? The basic concept of Zuczug/ is to establish the close and yet balanced relationship between life and design, and to promote an awareness of equality in the fashion industry. So, we insist on using ordinary people as our brand ambassadors, without using the 'idealized' picture of professional models. We give attention to life itself, and design different collections for different lifestyles. I believe that the most valuable and meaningful part of design is creating a garment from an individual perspective, knowing that it will be produced for and judged by the wider world.

How do you incorporate traditional Chinese culture in your designs? Zuczug/ believes that traditional culture can appear in contemporary design in an invisible and modern way, through shape, size, colour and space. There are also more direct ways to bring traditions into design, such as in our 'Nothing' collection (a collection related to the twelve animals in Chinese tradition).

Can you talk about the nature of Zuczug/ as a collective, with many contributors? Zuczug/ has developed into a hodgepodge of various designers. Every part of the brand has a chief designer in charge: Wu Weijia, Xin Yuan, Wang Yanyan, Kuang Ning, and we hope each part can carry the character of its chief designer. This 'assembly of individuality' is an important characteristic of Zuczug/.

Why has the brand been so successful in China? Certainly the collective nature of the brand has been instrumental, plus our independent values. In addition to this, my partner Huang Zhifeng and the entire team's efforts have been indispensable.

What do you look for when you are recruiting your design team? My first requirement for designers is to have individuality; the second one is to be open and be able to continue studying and cooperate with others. For me, communication is also a process of learning and knowing myself better.

Why do you think the world is now taking notice of contemporary Chinese designers and brands? This is related to China's rapid social, commercial and cultural development in the past few years. Judged by Western standards, the Chinese fashion industry is still relatively immature. However, Chinese designers and brands are enjoying a period of unprecedented opportunities, including the development of the Chinese consumer market and access to new technologies. I can feel the vitality in the Chinese fashion industry today.

Could you talk about your customer base? Zuczug/ has a group of stable customers, but this past year the Chinese fashion market has experienced a violent upheaval and significant changes, so we need to continue to attract new customers.

Do you engage with the next generation of designers? I used to lecture at university and now sometimes I return to campus to give speeches. I like the environment of my campus very much. Compared to the past, students are more independent and have better self-awareness, and those are good trends.

2013
白蛇传
第三回
ZUCZUG/forU + moretime

Page 249: 'Baishezhuan' collection, 2013.
Opposite: SS13.
This page: AW13.

This page and opposite: Catwalk, Shanghai
Fashion Week, AW12.

'We hope that traditional
culture can appear in
modern designs'

DIRECTORY

BABYGHOST
www.mybabyghost.com

BAN XIAOXUE
www.banxiaoxue.net

BOUNDLESS
boundlessboundless@163.com

CHICTOPIA
www.chictopia.net

CHRISTOPHER BU
www.christopherbu.com

COMME MOI
info@commemoi.com.cn

DEEPMOSS
www.deepmoss.com

DIGEST DESIGN
www.digest-design.com

EVENING
http://eveningyu.com

EXCEPTION DE MIXMIND
www.mixmind.com.cn

FAKE NATOO
fakenatoo307@163.com

FFIXXED
www.ffixxed.com

GUO PEI
www.rosestudio.com.cn

HAIZHEN WANG
www.haizhenwang.co.uk
studio@haizhenwang.co.uk

HE YAN
www.heyan.org
heyantutu@icloud.com

HELEN LEE
www.helenleefashion.com

HUISHAN ZHANG
huishanzhang.com

JNBY
www.jnby.com

LA CHAMBRE MINIATURE
www.lachambreminiature.com

LAURENCE XU
www.laurencexu.com

MASHA MA
www.masha-ma.com

MS MIN
http://msmin.com

NICOLE ZHANG
www.nicolezhang.com

POESIA BY CHRIS CHANG
http://poesiaworld.com/web

QIU HAO
www.qiuhaoqiuhao.com

RANFAN
www.ranfanstyle.com

RENLI SU
www.renlisu.com

RICOSTRU
www.ricostru.com

RYAN LO
www.ryanlo.co.uk

SANKUANZ
www.sankuanz.com

SEAN SUEN
www.seansuen.com

SHANG XIA
www.shang-xia.com

SIMONGAO
www.simon-gao.com

UMA WANG
www.umawang.com

VEGA ZAISHI WANG
www.vegawang.com

XANDER ZHOU
www.xanderzhou.com

XIAO LI
www.xiao-li.co.uk

YIFANG WAN
www.yf-wan.com

YIQING YIN
www.yiqingyin.com

YIRANTIAN
www.yirantian.com

ZUCZUG/
www.zuczug.com

All details correct at time of going to press.

PICTURE CREDITS

p.2 CHICTOPIA, SS14 Photo: Courtesy the designer.
p.7 XANDER ZHOU SS11. Photo: Trunk Xu, courtesy the designer.
p.9 MASHA MA, AW12 Photo: MatthieuBelin.com.
p.10 CHICTOPIA, Circus concept, SS12. Photo: MatthieuBelin.com.
p.12 Chen Man photo: Jing Yuke @Studio 6. Karchun Leung photo: Courtesy *Numéro China*.
p.13 Lucia Liu photo: Liu Song. Liu Wen photo: Justin Poland / The Society Management.
pp.14–15 Chris By Christopher Bu, 'Double' collection, SS14. Photo: Courtesy the designer.

BABYGHOST
pp.16, 18 Photo: Jonathan Waiter.
pp.19–21 Photo: Aingeru Zorita.

BAN XIAOXUE
pp.23–27 Photo: Courtesy the designer.

BOUNDLESS
pp. 28, 31 bottom right, 32–33 Photo: Zhuang Yan.
p.30 left Photo: Courtesy the designer.
p.30 right Photo: KA XiaoXi.
p.31 top left Photo: YangZi.

CHICTOPIA
pp.35–39 Photo: Courtesy the designer.

CHRISTOPHER BU
pp.40, 42–45 Photo: Courtesy the designer.

COMME MOI
pp.47–48 Photo: FengHai, model Lv Yan.
pp.49 and 50 left Singer Li Yuchun in Comme Moi, *Self* magazine. Photographer: Feng Hai.
p.50 right *Harper's Bazaar China* May 2014, photographer: Feng Hai, hair and makeup: Yue Hui, model: Du Juan.
p.51 Photo: Feng Hai, model Lv Yan.

DEEPMOSS
pp.53–54, 56–57 Photo: Zephyrance Lou.
p.55 Photo: XIAODONG XU-XD Studio.

DIGEST DESIGN
pp.59–63 Courtesy the designer.

EVENING
pp.64, 66–68 Photo WUQINXI.

EXCEPTION DE MIXMIND
pp.71, 75 EXCEPTION de MIXMIND in collaboration with Anothermountainman, Photo: Courtesy the designer.
pp.72–74 Courtesy the designer.

FAKE NATOO
p.77 Reclothing Bank, 2011.
pp.78–79, 81 Photo: Courtesy the designer.

FFIXXED
pp.82, 87 right Photo: Courtesy The Woolmark Company.
pp.85–87 Photography by Studio TM.

GUO PEI
p.88 Rose Studio Couture Co. Ltd.

p.90 left ROSLAN RAHMAN/AFP/Getty Images.
p.90 right © EDGAR SU/Reuters/Corbis.
p.91 China Photos/Getty Images.

HAIZHEN WANG
pp.92–93 Photo: Jamie Mcphee.
pp.94–95, 97 Catwalking.com.
p.96 Photo: Christopher Dadey.

HE YAN
pp.99–100 Courtesy the designer.
p.101 Photo: MatthieuBelin.com.

HELEN LEE
pp.102, 104–105 Awei Sun.
pp.106–107 Charles Guo.

HUISHAN ZHANG
p.108 Courtesy Huishan Zhang.
pp.110–113 Courtesy Huishan Zhang.

JNBY
pp.115–117 Courtesy the designer.

LA CHAMBRE MINIATURE
p.118 Photo: Fender Xu.
pp.120–121 Sketches by Hong Chang Courtesy the designer.
p.122 *Numéro China* (photo: Trunk Xu).
p.123 Courtesy the designer (photo: Jun).

LAURENCE XU
pp.124, 126–127 Courtesy the designer.

MASHA MA
pp.128, 130–131 Courtesy the designer (photo: LIKA).
pp.132–133 Courtesy the designer (photo: Filippo Fior).

MS MIN
p.135 Photo: MatthieuBelin.com.
pp.136–139 Courtesy the designer.

NICOLE ZHANG
p.140 Zenan Cai.
pp.143–144, 145 bottom left and right Roy Zhang.
p.145 top Jameski.

POESIA BY CHRIS CHANG
p.146 Giuseppe Cialoa.
p.148 Courtesy Shanghai Fashion Week.
p.149 Tanms Kung.
p.150, 151 bottom Ambrous Young.
p.151 top Fender Hsu.

QIU HAO
pp.152, 154–155 Photo: Yucong.
p.156 Photo: MatthieuBelin.com, image edited by Qiu Hao studio.
p.157 Likai.

RANFAN
pp.159–163 Photo: Courtesy the designer.

RENLI SU
pp.164, 166–167 Mariona Vilaros.
p.168 Raymond Tan.

p.169 Mariona Vilaros.

RICOSTRU
p.171 Photo: MatthieuBelin.com.
p.172 Allan Chui.
p.173 Courtesy the designer.
pp.174–175 Zeng Wu.

RYAN LO
p.176 Daniel Sims.
p.178 Catwalking.com.
pp.179–181 Ryan Lo Studio.

SANKUANZ
pp.182, 184–185 Sankuanz SS15 LCM Chris Yates 2014.
pp.186–187 Courtesy the designer.

SEAN SUEN
pp.188, 190, 192–193 Photo by Cong Yu.
pp.189, 191 Courtesy the designer (photo: Trunk Xu)

SHANG XIA
p.195 *Life* magazine. Photo: MatthieuBelin.com.
pp.196–199 Image: Paolo Roversi.

SIMONGAO
pp.200–205 Courtesy the designer.

UMA WANG
pp.206, 209–211 Courtesy the designer.

VEGA ZAISHI WANG
pp.212–217 Vega Zaishi Wang Studio. Photo: Siliang Ma.

XANDER ZHOU
pp.219–220 Trunk Xu.
p.221 Mari Sarai.
pp.222 top left, 222 bottom left Catwalking.com.
p.222 right Simon Armstrong.
p.223 Courtesy the designer.

XIAO LI
pp.224, 226, 227 left and top right, 228–229 Anya Holdstock.
p.227 bottom right Christopher Dadey.

YIFANG WAN
pp.230–231 *Life* magazine, MatthieuBelin.com.
pp.232–234 Courtesy the designer.
p.235 Photo: MatthieuBelin.com.

YIQING YIN
p.236 Nicolas Guerin.
pp.238, 240–241 Shoji Fujii.
p.239 Marthe Sobczak. Model: Alane @ Trends.

YIRANTIAN
pp.243–244, 246–247 Photographer: Shawn Chen. Model: Nina from Elite London.
p.245 Courtesy the designer.

ZUCZUG/
p.249 Photo: Zhang Hong.
p.250 Photo: COCA.
p.251 Photo: Yanglu
pp.252–253 Photo: Wang Jialun.

ACKNOWLEDGMENTS

This book could not have been written without the many acts of kindness (big and small) I received along the way.

Thank you to: Vicky Yang at the Society Management, James Hazlett-Beard, Shaun Beyen, Fenella Barber and the China British Business Council (CBBC), Jiang Zhou and Jeff Yu at Studio 6, Mina White at IMG, Aingeru Zorita, Xiao Wen Ju, Mesh Chhibber, Jean Wylie at Reuter PR, Ritchie Chan at Triple Major, Tang Shuang, Shen Shen Zeng at Brand New China, Tasha Liu and Charles Wang at Dong Liang, Patricia Lagrange and Pascale Duchemin at City Models, Adlie Hoxha and Jennifer Reidy at Next Models, Timothy Parent, Svante Jerling, Tom Griffiths and Stella Zheng at Hot Pot Digital, Rob Han, Leo Lui, Austin Gormley, Xiaoqin Wu, Paddy Wang, Jiancui, Vivien Mo and Stephanie Ng at Styleasta. com, Harriet Cherry at Artesta.com, Lou Lou Han and Leo Huang.

My warmest thanks to Professor Frances Corner OBE, Head of London College of Fashion and Pro Vice-Chancellor of University of the Arts London, for her generous support, which facilitated research in China.

I would also like to express my extreme gratitude to each participating designer and their teams for their endless support and enthusiasm for this publication, especially Claire Slinn, Jimmy Tang, Roxanne Peters, Vivian Wong, Li Pinjing, Donni Xu, Chris Mao, Jin Te, Hester Kitchen, Sun Yunzhong and Pia Lai, Semma Chan, Ian Hylton, Chao Wang, Emma He, Liza Li, Candice Wang, Justine Young, Axel Wang, Tan Yi, Yuting Chen, Chris Rekrutiak, Robyn Xu, Madeleine Davenport, Chen Yuxuan, Limin Yu, Diana Yi, Clara Lin, ShuShu Chen, Jessamine Low and Qiuyuan Zhang, Jerry Lo and Luna Shi.

Likewise, the book's panel and Huang Hung, for their useful insights and guidance. I would also like to thank all the photographers for their images, in particular Matthieu Belin for his continued help and evocative photography. Jenny Lawson, Lauren Necati and all the staff at Thames & Hudson were also hugely accommodating.

A massive debt of gratitude to my assistants, namely Chenyang Huang, Mo Shi, Minyue Shi and Gwendolin Barber for all their varied yet fantastic efforts. Dianting Jiang was extraordinary in her tireless support of this project and I also want to particularly thank my exemplary image researcher, Rafaelle Swynghedauw, whose work from the start was faultless. Finally my editor's belief in this project was instrumental throughout – thank you Laura Potter!

This book is dedicated to my parents.